**Harvard
Business
Review**

on

WINNING
NEGOTIATIONS

The Harvard Business Review
Paperback series

If you need the best practices and ideas for the business challenges you face—but don't have time to find them—*Harvard Business Review* **paperbacks** are for you. Each book is a collection of HBR's inspiring and useful perspectives on a given management topic, all in one place.

The titles include:

Harvard Business Review on Advancing Your Career
Harvard Business Review on Aligning Technology with
    Strategy
Harvard Business Review on Building Better Teams
Harvard Business Review on Collaborating Effectively
Harvard Business Review on Communicating Effectively
Harvard Business Review on Finding & Keeping the Best
    People
Harvard Business Review on Fixing Health Care from
    Inside & Out
Harvard Business Review on Greening Your Business
    Profitably
Harvard Business Review on Increasing Customer Loyalty
Harvard Business Review on Inspiring & Executing
    Innovation
Harvard Business Review on Making Smart Decisions
Harvard Business Review on Managing Supply Chains
Harvard Business Review on Rebuilding Your Business Model
Harvard Business Review on Reinventing Your Marketing
Harvard Business Review on Succeeding as an Entrepreneur
Harvard Business Review on Thriving in Emerging Markets
Harvard Business Review on Winning Negotiations

Harvard
Business
Review

on

WINNING
NEGOTIATIONS

Harvard Business Review Press

Boston, Massachusetts

Library of Congress Cataloging-in-Publication Data

Harvard business review on winning negotiations.
    p. cm. — (The Harvard business review paperback series)
    Contains articles previously published in the Harvard business review.
    ISBN 978-1-4221-6257-6 (alk. paper)
  1. Negotiation in business.   2. Negotiation.   I. Harvard business review.
    HD58.6.H385 2011
    658.4'052—dc22

                                                          2011000868

Contents

Investigative Negotiation 1
Deepak Malhotra and Max H. Bazerman

Deals Without Delusions 19
Dan Lovallo, Patrick Viguerie, Robert Uhlaner, and John Horn

Breakthrough Bargaining 39
Deborah M. Kolb and Judith Williams

Building Deals on Bedrock 63
David Harding and Sam Rovit

Getting Past Yes: Negotiating as if Implementation Mattered 85
Danny Ertel

Negotiating Without a Net: A Conversation with the NYPD's Dominick J. Misino 111
Diane L. Coutu

Six Habits of Merely Effective Negotiators 127
James K. Sebenius

The Fine Art of Friendly Acquisition 155
Robert J. Aiello and Michael D. Watkins

Negotiating the Spirit of the Deal 177
Ron S. Fortgang, David A. Lax, and James K. Sebenius

When to Walk Away from a Deal 205
Geoffrey Cullinan, Jean-Marc Le Roux, and Rolf-Magnus Weddigen

Index 231

Harvard Business Review

on

WINNING NEGOTIATIONS

Investigative Negotiation

by Deepak Malhotra and Max H. Bazerman

CHRIS, A *FORTUNE* 500 executive, is known in his firm as a gifted negotiator who can break impossible deadlocks. Consider his performance in the following deal.

A few years ago, Chris's company entered into negotiations with a small European firm to buy an ingredient for a new health care product. (Some details have been changed to protect the companies involved.) The two sides settled on a price of $18 a pound for a million pounds of the substance annually. However, a disagreement developed over terms. The European supplier refused to sell the ingredient exclusively to the U.S. firm, and the U.S. firm was unwilling to invest in a product that was based on an ingredient its competitors could easily acquire. With considerable hesitation, the U.S. negotiators sweetened the deal, offering guaranteed minimum orders and a higher price. To their shock, the supplier still balked at providing exclusivity—even though it had no chance of selling anything close to a million pounds a year to anyone else. The negotiation seemed to be at a dead end, with the U.S. negotiators out of ideas for pushing through a deal. Even worse, the relationship had deteriorated so much that neither side trusted the other to continue bargaining in good faith.

At that point the stymied U.S. team brought in Chris to help improve relations. He did more than that. After listening to the facts, he asked the Europeans a simple question: Why? *Why* wouldn't they provide exclusivity to his corporation, which would buy as much of the ingredient as they could produce? The response surprised the Americans. Exclusivity would require the supplier's owner to violate an agreement with his cousin, who bought 250 pounds of the ingredient each year to make a locally sold product. Armed with this new knowledge, Chris proposed a solution that allowed the two firms to quickly wrap up a deal. The European firm would provide exclusivity with the exception of a few hundred pounds annually for the supplier's cousin.

In retrospect, that solution seems obvious. But as we've seen in real-world negotiations, as well as in classroom simulations with seasoned deal makers, this type of problem solving is exceedingly rare. That's because most negotiators wrongly assume that they understand the other side's motivations and, therefore, don't explore them further. The U.S. team members initially failed because they thought they knew why the supplier was being difficult: Clearly, they assumed, the Europeans were holding out for a higher price or didn't want to lose out on future deals with other customers.

Would you have made the same mistake? We have presented this case to hundreds of experienced executives

Idea in Brief

You've just asked a supplier for exclusive rights to a new ingredient for a product you intend to market globally. He balks. You sweeten the deal by offering a higher price. But he still won't budge.

You could assume the situation's hopeless and walk away. However ... you decide instead to ask *why* the supplier won't provide exclusivity. He says another buyer needs a tiny amount of the ingredient for a locally sold product. You propose exclusivity with the exception of this small amount. The supplier agrees.

You've just practiced **investigative negotiation,** recommended by Malhotra and Bazerman. To be an effective negotiator, focus less on selling your position on the issue at hand. Instead, pose questions to uncover information about the other party's constraints, interests, and priorities. Armed with that data, you'll expand agreement options. And you'll forge far more successful deals.

in negotiation courses at Harvard Business School. When we asked them to strategize on behalf of Chris's team about how to break the impasse, roughly 90% of their answers sounded like these: "Consent to a larger minimum purchase agreement." "Ask for a shorter exclusivity period." "Buy out the supplier." "Increase your offer price." "Threaten to walk away." All those suggestions share the same flaw: They are solutions to a problem that has not been diagnosed. Moreover, even if one of them had been effective in securing exclusivity, it would have been more costly than Chris's solution.

Chris succeeded because he challenged assumptions and gathered critical information regarding the other party's perspective—the first step in what we call "investigative negotiation." This approach, introduced in our new book, *Negotiation Genius,* entails both a mind-set and a methodology. It encourages negotiators to enter

Idea in Practice

Malhotra and Bazerman delineate five principles of investigative negotiation:

Ask why the other side wants what it wants.

Don't just discuss *what* your counterparts want; find out *why* they want it. By asking this question, you uncover a wider range of options for crafting a mutually satisfying deal.

Mitigate the other party's constraints.

Collaborating on solutions to other parties' concerns can prevent their problems from becoming your problems once a deal is implemented.

> *Example:* After a manufacturer had negotiated an order with a parts supplier that specified delivery within three months, the supplier seemed uneasy about the delivery deadline. Realizing that a delivery delay would cost her

company $1 million, the manufacturer offered to accept a potential delay if the supplier dropped his price by that amount. He refused. She asked, "Why can't you cheaply manufacture the parts in three months?" He said: "We can—but we can't cheaply ship the order to arrive on time." The manufacturer had favorable terms with a shipping company and offered to have it deliver the parts in 2.5 months. The supplier agreed to pay shipping costs and drop his price by $.5 million.

Interpret demands as opportunities.

Consider what seemingly unreasonable demands suggest about the other party's needs and interests.

> *Example:* A builder and developer were negotiating a contract. When the

talks the same way a detective enters a crime scene: by learning as much as possible about the situation and the people involved.

Though the solution to every negotiation may not be as straightforward as Chris's, his approach can help in even the most complex deals. In this article, we delineate five principles underlying investigative negotiation and show how they apply in myriad situations.

developer demanded the builder pay large penalties if the project fell behind schedule, the builder speculated that the developer might value early completion. He proposed paying even higher penalties if the project was delayed but suggested the developer pay him a bonus if he finished ahead of schedule. They sealed the deal.

Create common ground with adversaries.

Don't assume that your industry competitors are always adversaries. Consider them as potential allies in negotiations with a common third party.

Example: Two pharmaceutical companies wanted to buy eggs from a supplier. One needed 80,000 eggs; the other, 70,000. But the supplier had only 100,000 eggs. Through discussion, the companies realized their needs were complementary. One needed egg whites; the other, yolks. They split the cost of the eggs, each taking what they needed.

Investigate even if the deal seems lost.

New information may help you save a seemingly unsuccessful negotiation.

Example: A manufacturing CEO learned a prospect had decided to purchase from a competitor. She asked the prospect's VP why. He said the competitor, despite charging more, included product features he valued. She had assumed he cared mostly about price so had originally offered a barebones low-cost deal. She revised her offer to give him the best price and competition-beating features. Her prospect accepted.

Principle 1: Don't Just Discuss *What* Your Counterparts Want—Find Out *Why* they Want It

This principle works in fairly straightforward negotiations, like Chris's, and can be applied fruitfully to complex multiparty negotiations as well. Consider the dilemma facing Richard Holbrooke in late 2000, when he was the U.S. ambassador to the United Nations.

At the time, the United States was more than $1 billion in arrears to the UN but was unwilling to pay it unless the UN agreed to a variety of reforms. As a result, U.S. representatives were being sidelined in UN committee meetings, and the country faced losing its vote in the General Assembly. Meanwhile, U.S. senators were calling for a withdrawal from the organization.

Why the turmoil? For decades the United States had paid 25% of the regular UN budget. Believing that was too large a share, Congress decided to hold the $1 billion hostage until the UN agreed to, among other changes, reduce the U.S. assessment from 25% to 22% of the budget. The other UN member states saw this as a nefarious tactic.

Ambassador Holbrooke faced a tough challenge. According to UN regulations, a change in the allocation of dues needed the approval of all 189 members. What's more, a hard deadline was fast approaching. The Helms-Biden bill, which had appropriated close to $1 billion to cover much of what the United States owed, stipulated that if a deal was not struck by January 1, 2001, the money would disappear from the federal budget.

Holbrooke's team had hoped that Japan and some European countries would absorb most of the U.S. reductions. Unfortunately, the Japanese (who were already the second-highest contributors) rejected that idea outright. The Europeans also balked. How could Holbrooke break the impasse?

With the clock ticking, he and his team decided to concentrate less on persuading member states of the need for change and more on better understanding their perspectives. Whenever a member resisted an increase, Holbrooke, instead of arguing, would push further to discover precisely why it could not (or would not) pay more. Soon, one entirely unanticipated reason became salient: Many countries that might otherwise agree to increase their contributions did not have room to do so in their 2001 budgets, because they had already been finalized. The January 1 deadline was making the deal unworkable.

This new understanding of the problem gave rise to a possible solution. Holbrooke's proposal was to immediately reduce U.S. assessments from 25% to 22% to meet Congress's deadline but delay the increase in contributions from other nations until 2002. (The 2001 shortfall was covered by CNN founder and philanthropist Ted Turner, who agreed to make a onetime personal contribution of $34 million to the UN.) The key to resolving the conflict, however, was discovering that the dispute entailed not one issue but two: the timing of assessments as well as their size. Once the negotiators broadened their focus to include the issue of the timing, they could strike a deal that allowed each side to get what it wanted on the issue it cared about most.

Principle 2: Seek to Understand and Mitigate the Other Side's Constraints

Outside forces can limit our ability to negotiate effectively. We may be constrained by advice from lawyers, by corporate policies that prohibit making concessions, by fear of setting a dangerous precedent, by obligations to other parties, by time pressure, and so on. Similarly, the other side has constraints that can lead it to act in ways that don't seem rational—and that can destroy value for both sides—but unfortunately, the constraints of the other side are often hidden from (or ignored by) us.

Smart negotiators attempt to discover the other party's constraints—and to help overcome them—rather than dismiss the other side as unreasonable or the deal as unworkable. Above all, investigative negotiators never view the other side's constraints as simply *"their* problem."

The experience of a company we'll call HomeStuff demonstrates why. At HomeStuff, a producer of household appliances, the CEO was negotiating the purchase of mechanical parts from a supplier we'll call Kogs. The two key issues were price and delivery date. HomeStuff wanted to pay a low price and get immediate delivery; Kogs sought a high price and more time to deliver the goods.

Eventually, the parties agreed on a price of $17 million and delivery within three months. "Meeting that deadline will be difficult for me," said the supplier, "but I'll manage." The CEO of HomeStuff was tempted to let the discussion end there—the deal was already done and meeting the deadline was now the supplier's problem—but she decided to explore matters further. Aware that a delivery after three months would cost her company close to $1 million, she offered to accept a delay if Kogs would drop the price by that amount. "I appreciate the offer," the supplier responded, "but I can't accommodate such a large price cut."

Curious, the CEO pressed on. "I'm surprised that a three-month delivery would be so costly to you," she said to the supplier. "Tell me more about your production process so that I can understand why you can't cheaply manufacture the parts in that time frame." "Ah! But that's not the problem," the supplier explained. "We can easily manufacture the products in three months. But we have no way of cheaply shipping the order so it would arrive on time."

When the HomeStuff CEO heard this, she was thrilled. Because her firm often had to transport products quickly, it had arranged favorable terms with a shipping company. Using that service, HomeStuff could have the parts delivered in *less than* three months for a small fraction of what the supplier would have paid.

The CEO made the following offer, which the supplier immediately accepted: HomeStuff would arrange for its own shipper to deliver the parts in two and a half months, the supplier would pay the shipping costs, and the price would drop from $17 million to $16.5 million.

As this story illustrates, the other side's problem can quickly become your own. This is true not only when the other party is quietly accepting its constraints but also when it's being disagreeable. Often, when the other side refuses to meet demands, its intransigence is interpreted as a sure sign it's acting in self-interest, but in fact its hands may be tied. Through investigation, negotiators may find that they can help mitigate the other side's constraints to their own advantage.

Getting Information from Distrustful Negotiators

Negotiation entails risk

If you share private information with the people on the other side, they might use it to their advantage. Guess what? The other side feels the same way. When other parties seem to be hiding information and evading your questions, you are likely to see them as deceptive or conniving rather than simply nervous and afraid. Try giving them the benefit of the doubt, recognizing that most people are reluctant to open up in negotiations because they don't know whether you can be trusted. The following three tactics can help you elicit information when trust is in short supply.

Share information and encourage reciprocity

If you are up against a reticent negotiator, be the first to share information, making it clear that you expect reciprocity. For example, you might say: "I know that there are many things we need to discuss. If you prefer, I can get the ball rolling by describing some of my key interests, concerns, and constraints. Then you can do the same. Does that sound like a reasonable way to proceed?" Such an approach helps reduce the other side's anxiety, because the other party knows that both sides will be vulnerable.

Keep in mind two things. First, you want to explicitly state the ground rules up front: I will start, and then you will follow suit.

Principle 3: Interpret Demands as Opportunities

The CEO of a successful construction company was negotiating a deal to build a number of midsize office buildings. After months of talks—but just before the contract was signed—the developer approached the CEO with an

Make sure that the other side commits to reciprocating. Second, if the parties don't have full confidence in each other, share information incrementally, taking turns with the other side. That minimizes your own risks. If the other party fails to be forthcoming, you can hold back.

Negotiate multiple issues simultaneously

In most complex negotiations, issues are discussed one at a time. You might start by discussing what's presumed to be the most important (for example, price). When you have reached some agreement on price, you turn your attention to another concern (such as contract length), and then another (such as exclusivity). However, when there is only one issue on the table at any given moment, both sides behave as if it is the most important issue to them. When you move to the second concern, that concern appears to be the most critical. And so you continue to clash on each issue and never learn what the other party truly values or needs most.

Often, it's better to negotiate multiple issues simultaneously. That is, identify all the issues up front and put everything on the table at the same time. Then, go back and forth between the issues as you make offers and counteroffers. Doing so allows you to get information regarding the other side's true interests and priorities.

entirely new and potentially costly demand: a clause that would require the builder to pay large penalties if the project fell more than one month behind schedule. The CEO, understandably, was irritated by this last-minute attempt to squeeze more concessions from him.

The builder weighed his options. He could accept the new clause and seal the deal, he could reject it and hope

Getting Information from Distrustful Negotiators (continued)

To determine what is really most important to the other side, look at the following signs:

- Which issue does the other party want to return to constantly?
- Which issue makes him or her the most emotional, tense, or stressed?
- Which issues are most likely to lead your counterpart to try to control the conversation, rather than listen?
- What is the other side most obstinate about when you ask for a concession or compromise?

Make multiple offers at the same time

Not only is it useful to negotiate multiple issues simultaneously, but it is also useful to make multiple *offers* at once. The next time you are preparing to make an offer to the other side, stop. Instead, make two offers at the same time that are equally valuable to you but differ on the details of one pair of issues.

Consider the case of a business owner who was negotiating with an ex-employee. The ex-employee was threatening to sue for having been fired without cause. The business owner preferred to settle out of court and soon discovered that the ex-employee was offering to settle for $15,000 in cash plus six months of temporary employer-paid health insurance. The business owner felt this

the deal would survive, or he could try to negotiate lower penalties. As he thought more deeply, he began to focus less on possible responses and more on what the demand revealed. At the very least, it showed that the developer had a strong interest in timely project completion. But might it also suggest that the developer valued *early* completion? With that in mind, the CEO amount was unjustified but was willing to negotiate. He started by asking whether the ex-employee cared more about the cash or about the health coverage. The ex-employee refused to offer this information. The business owner, having first calculated that the cost of providing the insurance would be approximately $2,500 for three months, decided to propose two options.

Offer X: $7,500 plus three months of health insurance.

Offer Y: $5,000 plus six months of health insurance.

The ex-employee was unwilling to accept either of the offers outright but voiced a preference for something closer to Y than X. This revealed that health insurance was more valuable to him than the cash. Offering him two options had prompted him to divulge his relative preferences. The final arrangement, then, could be made more attractive to the ex-employee and less costly to the business owner if further concessions were more heavily weighted toward insurance than toward cash.

Making multiple offers simultaneously is a great tactic for other reasons as well. It allows you to discover the interests of reticent negotiators, and it also makes you appear flexible and empathetic. It signals to the people on the other side that you are willing to be accommodating and interested in understanding their needs.

approached the developer with a new proposal: He would pay even higher penalties than the developer wanted if the project was delayed. If the project was completed earlier than scheduled, however, the developer would give the construction company a bonus. Both sides agreed to that clause and were happier with the new terms. The builder was confident that his company would finish ahead of schedule and receive the bonus, and the developer minimized his downside risk.

Typically, when the other side makes seemingly unreasonable demands, negotiators adopt a defensive mind-set: "How can I avoid having to accept this?" In contrast, investigative negotiators confront difficult demands the same way they confront any statement from the other party: "What can I learn from the other side's insistence on this issue? What does this demand tell me about this party's needs and interests? How can I use this information to create and capture value?" The construction company CEO's breakthrough came from his ability to shift his efforts away from fighting the other side's demand and toward investigating the opportunities hidden beneath it.

Principle 4: Create Common Ground with Adversaries

Negotiation professors often engage their students in a complex simulation called "The Commodity Purchase," written by Leonard Greenhalgh of Dartmouth's Tuck School of Business. In it, one student plays the role of the seller of 100,000 pheasant eggs, and five other students play potential egg buyers. The buyers have different motives (for example, some want chemicals in the eggs to manufacture health products) and need a variety of quantities, encouraging the formation of coalitions among them. The alliance that will create the most value, however, involves two competing pharmaceutical firms that, by cooperating, have the potential to outbid the other three buyers. The problem is that one of the firms needs at least 80,000 eggs, the other needs at least 70,000, and it is not obvious how both can get what they want, given that there are only 100,000 eggs. In fact, only about 5% of MBA students and executives that participate in this simulation manage to discover the solution.

To find it the company reps must first realize that the needs of their respective pharmaceutical firms are complementary, not competitive. Specifically, one firm needs the whites of the eggs, and the other needs the yolks. Once they know this, the two firms can split the cost of the eggs and each take what they need from the acquired product. However, few come to this conclusion, because to develop it the parties must adopt an investigative negotiation approach, overcome their reluctance to seek common ground with someone who is considered the enemy, and attempt to understand their competitor's perspective. The naive assumption that other firms in the same industry are strictly competitors typically prevents negotiators from taking an investigative approach.

As professors Adam Brandenburger of New York University and Barry Nalebuff of Yale University demonstrate in their book *Co-opetition,* it is often possible to simultaneously cooperate and compete with others. Investigative negotiators understand this. Those who view their relationship with the other side as one-dimensional—"He is my competitor"—forgo opportunities for value creation, whereas those who appreciate the complexity of relationships and explore areas of mutual interest are able to find common ground.

Principle 5: Continue to Investigate Even After the Deal Appears to be Lost

How many times have you tried to close a deal only to have your final offer rejected? If you are like most people, once someone has said no to your best offer, you presume there is nothing left to do. Often, this is the case. Sometimes, however, you are wrong—and you lose the deal not because there was no viable agreement but because you did not negotiate effectively.

A few years ago the chief executive of a specialty-gift-item manufacturer learned that a *Fortune* 500 company she had courted for months had decided to purchase from her competitor. Though she had no further plans for winning the deal, the CEO placed one final call to the prospect's vice president, asking why her offer was rejected and explaining that an answer could help her improve future offerings.

To the CEO's surprise, the VP explained that the competitor, despite charging more, had beaten her offer by including product features that his company valued. Under the false assumption that the prospect cared mostly about price, the CEO had made a final offer that reduced the prospect's cost as much as possible. The CEO thanked the VP for his explanation and added that she had misunderstood his position earlier. "Knowing what I know now," she told him, "I'm confident that I could have beaten their offer. Would you consider a revised offer?" The answer was yes. One week later the CEO won over the prospect—and signed the deal.

After being rejected, an investigative negotiator should immediately ask, "What would it have taken for us to reach agreement?" Though it may appear costly to continue negotiating when a "no deal" response appears certain, if you're confused about the *reason* your deal fell through in the first place, it could be even more costly to abandon the discussion.

Even if you find that you cannot win the deal, you may still acquire important information that will help in future negotiations. By staying at the table, you can learn about this customer's future needs, the interests and concerns of similar customers, or the strategies of other players in the industry. Keep in mind that it is often easier to get candid information from the other side when you are not in selling mode and there is little reason to distrust your motives. Next time you've lost the deal and been asked to leave the room, see if you can stick around and investigate further. You may be surprised by what you find out.

As these five principles demonstrate, successful investigative negotiation requires challenging some time-honored negotiation approaches. Chief among these is the reflex to "sell" your position.

Imagine that you're observing a salesperson at work. What is he doing? Most people picture a smooth talker with a briefcase making a pitch—arguing his case and trying to persuade a potential target to buy what he has to offer. Now imagine that you're observing a negotiator at work. What is he doing? If, once again, you picture a smooth talker with a briefcase making a pitch, you are missing a crucial distinction between selling and negotiating.

Selling involves telling people about the virtues of your products or services, focusing on the strengths of your case, and trying to induce agreement or compliance. While effective negotiating requires some of those activities, as the previous cases demonstrate, it also requires a strong focus on the other side's interests, priorities, and constraints. Investigative negotiators— like truly effective salespeople—keep this focus top of mind. They also understand that constructing a value-maximizing deal often hinges not on their ability to persuade but on their ability to listen.

In the end, negotiation is an information game. Those who know how to obtain information perform better than those who stick with what they know. In the situations described here, the decision to challenge assumptions, probe below the surface, and avoid taking no for an answer helped negotiators improve their options and strike better deals. More generally, the investigative negotiation approach can help you transform competitive negotiations into ones with potential for building trust and cooperation, creating value, and engendering mutual satisfaction.

DEEPAK MALHOTRA is an associate professor of business administration. **MAX H. BAZERMAN** is the Jesse Isidor Straus Professor of Business Administration at Harvard Business School.

Originally published in September 2007. Reprint R0709D

Deals Without Delusions

by Dan Lovallo, Patrick Viguerie, Robert Uhlaner, and John Horn

IF YOUR FIRM IS LOOKING to acquire, how can you tell whether a given deal is advantageous? Unfortunately, you can never be sure that any large organic or acquisition investment will pay off, which may explain why many firms shy away from purchases that might otherwise afford them important growth opportunities. The good news is that you can stack the odds in your favor by examining a psychological phenomenon that most executives never consider when making deals—the degree to which their own biases influence decisions.

Before we disentangle the biases, let's consider some facts about M&A nowadays. A typical large corporation derives 30% of its revenue growth through acquisitions. For a $10 billion company growing by 10% annually, that's $300 million in revenues a year. Our work has shown that companies that aggressively leverage acquisitions for growth are at least as successful in the eyes of the capital markets as those that focus on purely organic ways to grow. Nevertheless, recent research from McKinsey & Company reveals that approximately half of acquiring companies continue to pay more for acquisitions than they're worth. Certainly, firms are getting better at M&A—2006 was almost a ten-year high in the percentage of shareholder value created through takeovers—but there's still plenty of room for improvement.

Many scholars have attributed the largest M&A mistakes to executive hubris in decision making, but having studied the psychology of the deal for over a decade, we believe this is only a small piece of the problem. Our insights have been confirmed by a recent McKinsey survey of executives responsible for M&A at 19 top U.S. firms. Each firm had derived at least 30% of its market value from acquisitions; the market rewarded some of these companies (their returns to shareholders exceeded those of peer firms) but did not reward others. Our analysis of responses from executives at these firms demonstrates how a variety of cognitive biases—systematic errors in processing information and making choices—can affect each step of the M&A process.

As we will show, when executives take a *targeted debiasing* approach to M&A, deals can be more successful. The approach requires executives first to identify the cognitive mechanisms at play during various decision-making steps and then to use a set of techniques to reduce bias at specific decision points, thereby leading to sounder judgments. (See the exhibit "How to overcome biases that undermine the M&A process.")

Idea in Brief

Half of all acquiring companies pay more for target firms than they're worth. Often it's because of executives' mental biases: Their interest in a deal keeps them from being objective about its value. Thus, during *preliminary due diligence,* many aspiring acquirers overestimate revenue and cost synergies. While *bidding,* they get sucked into price wars. And in the *final phase*—additional due diligence with access to the target's books—they ignore signals suggesting danger ahead.

To avoid overpaying for M&As, say Lovallo and his coauthors,

systematically attack mental bias. For instance, during due diligence, seek out evidence that challenges your assumptions about revenue and cost synergies. Don't bid until you've set a maximum price. And solicit independent analysts' perspectives during the final phase.

By anticipating and countering common mental biases, you make sounder judgments at each stage of the M&A process. You forge the right M&A deals—and steer clear of the wrong ones.

Preliminary Due Diligence: Five Biases

The preliminary due diligence stage of the M&A process is when biases are most likely to cause damage. They can, for example, lead a potential acquirer to overestimate enhancements to stand-alone values as well as revenue and cost synergies between the acquirer and the target. In addition, they can cause a deal maker to underestimate the challenge of integrating two corporate cultures. In this section, we explore five biases that tend to surface during preliminary due diligence. We also provide strategies for overcoming them and thereby avoiding their potentially costly consequences.

Idea in Practice

The authors suggest strategies for countering mental biases at each stage of the M&A process.

Preliminary Due Diligence

Confirmation bias—seeking out information that validates your initial interest in the target company.

Antidote: Seek evidence disconfirming your estimates of the deal's potential value.

> *Example:* A company looking to acquire a firm with a complementary technology takes into account the target's slowing growth rates—which signal deteriorating attractiveness of the target's markets.

Overconfidence—relying solely on your own estimates of synergies between your firm and the target.

Antidote: Examine numerous similar deals your firm and others have done. If your expected synergies are skewed toward the high end of, or beyond, what comparable deals have yielded, watch out.

Underestimating cultural differences—ignoring conflicts between merging firms' cultural conventions that can damage post-M&A performance.

Antidote: Identify potential problems, such as differences between compensation systems, and develop plans for addressing them.

Confirmation Bias

People have an overwhelming tendency to seek out information that validates an initial hypothesis. This bias is particularly pernicious during M&A preliminary due diligence, because the main outcome is a letter of intent (LOI) with a price range that's enticing enough to move a deal forward. The need to provide an acceptable initial bid often biases all analyses upward. Instead of synergy estimates guiding the price, as would be appropriate, the LOI often guides the synergy estimates. In effect, this seeds the entire due diligence process with a biased

Underestimating time, money, and other resources needed for integration.

Antidote: Identify best practices for improving integration efforts.

Example: GE Capital applies Six Sigma principles to drive continuous improvement in its integration practices and sponsors conferences to foster idea sharing on M&As.

Bidding

Bidding above the target's true value when multiple players enter the game.

Antidotes: Set a maximum price for each deal. Then walk away if competitors initiate a bidding war.

Final Due Diligence

Anchoring—refusing to adjust an initial valuation even if new information about the target firm suggests that the initial number is meaningless.

Sunk costs fallacy—refusing to walk away from the deal, even if the costs are unrecoverable, because you've invested so much time, money, effort, and reputation into making the deal happen.

Antidotes: Hire fresh, dispassionate experts to examine relevant aspects of the deal—but don't tell them your initial estimate of the deal's value. Always entertain multiple M&A possibilities; you won't get so emotionally attached to one deal.

estimate, even before much factual information has been exchanged.

During the price-setting stage, deal makers also sometimes use current market multiples as evidence to confirm the wisdom of a deal, in lieu of a compelling business case. In 2003, for example, Career Education Corporation (CEC) paid $245 million—14 times its annual operating earnings—for Whitman Education Group. (The historical multiple in this industry is six to eight times earnings.) CEC executives justified the high price by arguing that the sector was undergoing a period in which high prices were the norm. This convenient logic—in no way an independent test of the appropriate price—may explain why the executives opted to pay a high price, but it doesn't show whether that price *should* have been paid. Subsequently, stock prices for the industry receded to historical norms.

The best way to counteract confirmation bias is to tackle it head on—by actively seeking disconfirming evidence. Consider one company that did not do that. The firm sought to acquire a sizable firm that had a complementary technology. The acquirer hoped that the combined technology platform would enable significant new product development and fuel revenue growth. Since the quality of the technology was the driving force behind much of the due diligence, the acquirer didn't take into account the target's slowing growth rates, which should have signaled the deteriorating attractiveness of the target's markets. A harder look might have raised red flags earlier. Of course, most companies examine potential pitfalls at some point during the M&A process, but often not with the same degree of insight and strategic rigor that they build into their initial case for a deal.

Overconfidence

The ubiquitous problem of overconfidence is especially insidious when it comes to identifying revenue and cost synergies. Since revenue synergies are less likely to be realized than cost synergies are, heavy reliance on the former may signal a problem. For revenue synergies to work, there must be a specific integration plan that involves new investment in growth initiatives. This plan should

How to overcome biases that undermine the M&A process

At each step of the M&A process, executives can be vulnerable to a variety of cognitive biases. By identifying these biases and then taking specific steps to address them, deal makers can feel more comfortable with the process.

Process step	Bias	Debiasing prescriptions
Preliminary due diligence Estimate stand-alone enhancement, revenue synergies, and cost synergies; decide how much to bid; estimate the time, money, and other resources needed for integration.	Confirmation bias	Seek out disconfirming evidence.
	Overconfidence	Use a reference class of comparable prior deals to estimate synergies.
	Underestimation of cultural differences	Do human due diligence.
	Planning fallacy	Use reference-class forecasting to estimate the time and money needed for integration. Establish and update best practices.
	Conflict of interest	Seek advice from objective experts.
Bidding phase Submit bids until the seller agrees on a price.	Winner's curse	Set a limit price and avoid bidding wars. Have a dedicated M&A function.
Final phase Obtain greater access to the target's books; determine final payment terms and closing details.	Anchoring	Seek the fresh eyes of independent analysts.
	Sunk cost fallacy	Have backup plans and alternative options.

25

complement a balanced assessment of the entire competitive environment. One way to avoid overconfident synergy estimates is to use reference-class forecasting, which involves examining numerous similar deals that your firm and others have done, to see where the current deal falls within that distribution. It provides a top-down sanity check of typical bottom-up synergy estimates (see "Delusions of Success: How Optimism Undermines Executives' Decisions," HBR July 2003).

Leading serial acquirers, such as GE, Johnson & Johnson, and Cisco, draw from past experience when contemplating mergers. Companies that don't have rich M&A histories can often use analogous situations in other companies as benchmarks. To estimate synergies, firms look at a detailed business case from the bottom up; they also make top-down estimates on the basis of comparable deals. Recently, a banking firm examined more than a dozen comparable deals on three continents to make an accurate assessment of realized synergies. It is not necessary to calculate the exact value of the synergies in comparable deals; grouping them into a few performance categories—good, bad, or disastrous, for example—often suffices. Watch out if your firm's expected synergies are skewed toward the high end of, or beyond, what comparable deals have yielded and your performance with your current assets is not similarly skewed (see the sidebar "Eight Red Flags in M&A").

Underestimation of Cultural Differences
Unanticipated cultural conflicts are well known to cause merger problems; less well known is the idea that

Eight Red Flags in M&A

COMPANIES SHOULD BE VIGILANT for red flags during the M&A process. The presence of one flag does not necessarily signal certain danger, but spotting several probably means that peril is just around the corner.

- The CEO is the only one who believes in the deal.

- The synergies analysis focuses on revenue enhancement (without an investment plan) rather than cost savings.

- Preliminary cultural due diligence is done in a perfunctory manner.

- The acquirer has done few deals and hasn't sought outside expertise.

- The limit price changes during the bidding.

- There are numerous bidders for the target.

- At any stage of the process, someone emphasizes how much time, money, or reputation has already been sunk into the deal.

- You consider the deal to be one that you must close no matter what.

conflict can arise even in the most anodyne situations. In a simulation experiment performed in 2003, Roberto Weber and Colin Camerer showed how conflict between merging firms' cultural conventions (the codes, symbols, anecdotes, and rules that bind cultures together) can substantially diminish performance. Participants were assigned to either an acquiring or an acquired firm and given time to develop, within each group, a common language for describing generic photos of employees doing various kinds of work. When the firms were "merged," participants from the acquiring company who role-played as managers were able to communicate much more effectively with subordinate participants from their own firm than with those from the other firm. Sometimes, the person in the manager role grew impatient with the subordinate from the acquired company. The researchers concluded that "the more deeply ingrained firm-specific language is, and the more efficient the firm, the harder the integration may be." They also noted that employees of both the target and the acquirer tended to overestimate the performance of the combined firm and to attribute any diminished collective performance to members of the other firm—outcomes that are often evident in real-world mergers.

One way to prevent cultural conflicts is to perform cultural due diligence (see "Human Due Diligence," HBR April 2007). According to the previously discussed McKinsey survey, companies that had been rewarded by the market were 40% more likely than unrewarded companies to perform this due diligence at least "most of the time." We have also found that network analysis maps, which describe the connections among people in an organization, provide some insight about the similarities between company cultures and can help identify the key people to be retained during integration. (See "A Practical Guide to Social Networks," HBR March 2005, and "How to Build Your Network," HBR December 2005.) For one pharmaceutical client, McKinsey used network analysis to identify whether the target's scientists really were world-class research leaders in the area where the acquirer wanted to build capabilities. The results showed that the target's scientists were not essential for doing cutting-edge research on a key chemical, so the client decided to build the skills organically.

We believe that network analysis holds huge promise for refining the work of cultural due diligence. In the future, companies will be able to use this method to help identify which types of networks are easiest to integrate. The analysis should highlight places where the target's network is dependent on too few key capabilities and may even shed light on the target's quality of work.

The Planning Fallacy

People have a tendency to underestimate the time, money, and other resources needed to complete major projects, including mergers and acquisitions. We believe that reference-class forecasting, mentioned in our discussion of the overconfidence bias, has great promise as a tool for anticipating how much time and money will be needed for M&A integration. The American Planning Association, a nonprofit organization that helps communities plan infrastructure projects, routinely recommends this type of forecasting, and it is used to plan infrastructure development throughout the UK and Switzerland.

Firms that are successful at integration also formally identify best practices and use them to improve future integration efforts. For example, GE Capital applies the principles of Six Sigma to drive continuous improvement in its integration practices, just as it does for its other core business processes. Started more than 20 years ago, this approach has developed as the company has faced challenges in its various acquisitions. The firm's executives discovered that mergers go more smoothly if integration begins early in the deal-making process and if detailed written plans include clear objectives that are to be met immediately after the deal closes. GE Capital also surveys its own employees and those of the other company to compare cultures, sets up structured meetings to address cultural integration, and works to solve actual business problems based on shared new understanding. Most important, the firm has put in place a process for learning from deal-making experience. It also sponsors conferences to foster idea sharing and improvement of best practices, and it constantly updates materials for leaders in the newly acquired company to use. This commitment to learning, codification, and continuous improvement has helped make GE Capital a world-class integrator across the globe.

Conflict of Interest

Although advisers generally earn more business if deals they work on actually go through, the good advisers understand that the best way to secure a reputation is to provide objective recommendations that stand the test of time. Firms that do deals infrequently should be especially careful to stay clear of people who are driven by one-shot profit motives. Building a network of trusted advisers who are interested in the long haul goes far toward avoiding the conflict-of-interest bias.

Conflict of interest is an even bigger concern when a deal sponsor in charge of due diligence evaluates a merger or acquisition without obtaining any external input. Recent research by Don Moore and colleagues indicates that the judgment of internal partisans, and even of external advisers, is unconsciously influenced by the roles they play. Accordingly, they are likely to reach the same conclusions as their sponsor, unintentional as that outcome may be.

Private equity firm partners have proved very successful at reviewing one another's deals to ensure analytically rigorous due diligence. Even more important, they practice humility—that is, they approach each deal as if they didn't know anything about the relevant industry, even though they may buy multiple companies within it. They ask for expert advice; they question anyone who's willing to talk; they listen genuinely to the answers they receive. Corporate buyers, on the other hand, usually evaluate deals episodically, and certainly less often than private equity firms' investment committees, which tend to have weekly rhythms. As a result, corporate boards and management teams do not develop the skills they need to critically evaluate deals. This results in a conservative bias either to kill most deals or to take management's word and provide a rubber stamp. If your firm does deals infrequently, consider seeking out objective external expertise beyond that of the advisers assisting on the deal. (Also see the sidebar "Aversion to M&A: Two Biases.")

The Bidding Phase: Avoiding the Winner's Curse

If there are multiple bidders for an M&A target, a well-documented phenomenon called the *winner's curse* can

Aversion to M&A: Two Biases

THIS ARTICLE FOCUSES ON THE dangers of undertaking mergers and acquisitions, but we don't mean to imply that organic growth is a surer bet. Many executives feel reluctant to pursue M&A because they incorrectly believe it is riskier than organic growth, even though the probability of success with internal ventures is objectively the same as with external ones. Accordingly, too many firms never avail themselves of M&A growth possibilities. Indeed, the tendency to do too few deals seems at least as prevalent as the tendency to pursue value-destroying ones. Aversion to M&A springs from two key biases: *loss aversion* and *comparative ignorance*. Loss aversion refers to fearing losses more acutely than desiring equivalent gains. In many experiments, Daniel Kahneman and Amos Tversky have shown that the psychological impact of a loss is about 2 to 2.5 times that of a gain. This means that to accept an even chance of losing $10, most people require an upside of $20 to $25. Often, the net effect of loss aversion is inaction.

In a clever experiment undertaken in 1995 in Berkeley, California, Craig R. Fox and Amos Tversky demonstrated comparative ignorance by showing that given a pair of betting options, people prefer the gamble that is comparatively less uncertain. Participants were asked to price bets on whether the temperature at a given time in San Francisco (a familiar city) or Istanbul (an unfamiliar one) was greater or less than 60 degrees Fahrenheit. Some priced bets on only one city; others priced bets on both. When comparing the two bets, participants were willing to pay over 50% more for the San Francisco gamble than for the Istanbul gamble. But when different groups were asked to price bets on only one city, they priced the gambles equally. Thus, comparative ignorance led them to value the familiar-city gamble more highly, even though it had an identical risk profile.

Loss aversion and comparative ignorance played a role in a potentially lucrative merger contemplated by a large pharmaceutical company. The target was a smaller biotech firm whose key research asset was a drug intended to enhance cognitive function, which was midway through clinical trials. The executive committee didn't feel it understood the potential outcomes of the drug as well as those of some internal prospects, so it asked the senior executive and the line manager leading the merger venture whether they'd be willing to bet their careers on the drug's market outcome. When the two very reasonably said no, the executive committee interpreted this as a lack of commitment to the merger and rejected the acquisition, even though the internal prospects were not subject to the same degree of risk evaluation.

The best way to overcome loss aversion is to aggregate a particular M&A decision within the larger portfolio of strategic choices and thereby mitigate the loss associated with a single poor outcome. To understand the power of aggregation, consider the following thought experiment. Imagine you will flip a coin: If it lands tails up, you lose $10,000. What is the lowest amount you would have to receive if the coin lands heads up to accept the gamble? Now imagine you own 20 of these gambles. What is the lowest amount you would have to receive for each heads-up to accept the bet? Did the value drop? If so, you understand the power of aggregation: The chance of overall loss becomes vanishingly small as the number of gambles rises. Over a significant time horizon, firms can undertake numerous investments. So long as the acquisition investments don't threaten the firm's viability, they should be considered a small part of a continuing gamble. A culture that fires someone (or threatens to do so) for one relatively small deal that doesn't pan out is a culture where even good deals don't get done, as in the pharmaceutical example above.

You can overcome comparative ignorance by taking a look at the actual returns your company has achieved on internal projects and the returns you and others have achieved on acquisitions. This baseline, objective measure of the two types of returns can be formulated using a reference class of at least eight similar deals that you or others have done. Reviewing ventures in this way will help reduce uncertainty about an acquisition's potential range of outcomes, minimizing the ambiguity inherent in an unfamiliar gamble.

come into play. Someone bids above an item's true value and thus is "cursed" by acquiring it. Bidding wars often lead to above-value offers.

One bidding war broke out recently over Guidant, which makes heart devices such as defibrillators, pacemakers, and stents. Johnson & Johnson offered Guidant shareholders $68 a share in late 2004, which wasn't much of a premium over the stock's trading price. In early 2005, though, reports of problems with some of Guidant's defibrillators began reaching the public. When J&J subsequently dropped its offer to $63 a share, Boston Scientific offered $72 a share in late 2005. The bids increased over a couple of days in January 2006, until Boston Scientific decided to make a bid so strong that it ended the contest: $80 a share (with a collar) and an agreement not to walk even if the government objected or further recalls came to light. Soon after the deal closed, however, additional product recalls were issued and the value of Boston Scientific's stock fell by about half, although this deal may have not been the only cause of the drop. Boston Scientific's failure to protect itself from future changes and its rushed offer to end the bidding war made it fall prey to the winner's curse. Of course, this doesn't mean the company won't derive value from the deal in the long term.

The previously discussed McKinsey survey suggested that successful acquirers are much more likely to exit when competitors initiate a bidding war: 83% of the rewarded companies withdrew at least sometimes, compared with only 29% of the unrewarded companies. Staying in a bidding war doesn't necessarily lead to a poor acquisition, but if your company doesn't evaluate whether to drop out when others enter the bidding, that's a red flag.

One technique for avoiding the winner's curse is to tie the compensation of the person responsible for the deal's price to the success of the deal—for example, to the percentage of estimated synergies realized. An even better strategy is to have a dedicated M&A function that actively generates alternatives to the deal under consideration and sets a limit price for each deal. (Companies that don't proactively maintain a deal pipeline are often forced to overpay for what seems to be their only alternative.) This method isn't a guarantee against the curse, since your maximum price still might be greater than the target's true value, but it can prevent you, in a fit of auction fever, from increasing your bid above the level you initially deem prudent.

If the acquiring firm's limit price changes during the bidding, someone in the firm should wave a warning flag and stop the negotiations. If the acquiring firm doesn't have a limit when it starts bidding, the bidder should be struck with the flagstaff.

The Final Phase: The Perils of Clinging Tightly

Once an initial bid is accepted, the acquirer has an important opportunity for additional due diligence, since it now has much greater access to the target's books. The final negotiation phase also encompasses the deal's legal structuring (for example, the exact composition of payment cash or stock). In this final phase of due diligence, the goal is to honestly evaluate the investment case in light of the more detailed information now available from the target. Two biases can come into play.

The first stems from a tendency to underreact to surprising news. A simplifying heuristic called *anchoring* is operative here. Specifically, people tend to anchor onto an initial number and then insufficiently adjust away from it, even if the initial number is meaningless. In a classic article in *Science* magazine from 1974, Amos Tversky and Daniel Kahneman described how anchoring works. In one experiment, subjects witnessed the spinning of a roulette-type wheel emblazoned with numbers from 1 to 100. Then the subjects were asked what percentage of African countries were members of the United Nations. The random numbers generated by the wheel biased the subjects' answers. For example, when the spun number was 10, the median answer was 25%; when the spun number was 65, the median answer was 45%.

Initial valuations, such as the price range in the LOI, can also act as anchors. Many acquirers fail to adjust sufficiently from a price, even in the face of surprising new evidence. For example, one energy company pursued a deal in part because the target had a futures contract with Enron. Even when Enron collapsed soon afterward, the would-be acquirer remained anchored to its original estimates of the deal's value. After the deal went through, it spent an additional $30 million—beyond an initial price of approximately $75 million—to keep the deal in play. The deal never succeeded because the acquirer eventually ran into its own problems with regulators. Likewise, anchoring can occur in the process of bidding. Confronted with unfavorable information, the acquirer may not lower the price sufficiently. It's rare to be able to bargain down the LOI price, so stepping away is almost always the only way to avoid paying too much.

When people feel that they've sunk a lot of time, money, effort, and reputation into making a deal happen, they aren't willing to surrender, even if the costs are unrecoverable. The *sunk cost fallacy* can cause an acquirer to continue pursuing the target even when it shouldn't. This phenomenon probably was operative in Boston Scientific's pursuit of Guidant.

The best way to free your firm from both final-phase biases is to hire fresh, dispassionate experts to examine the relevant aspects of the deal without divulging the initial estimate. Some private equity firms use this technique. The independent team simply is asked to make its evaluation of the new information uncovered during the detailed due diligence—data that were not available before the initial bid was accepted.

Just as important, your firm should always entertain multiple M&A possibilities as part of a broader backup plan, and should know when to stop bargaining and walk away. When you have multiple offers in play, you aren't emotionally attached to one deal. Having a few options on the table also allows you to shift to another deal with a better price-value ratio as the bargaining continues. Of course, the ability to juggle several options at once requires a disciplined, ongoing M&A process and the attention of a much larger M&A team.

M&A is a vital component of any company's growth options, but doing it well means identifying the red flags. Taking a targeted debiasing approach can help the acquiring team make better, more accurate value estimates and can help mitigate the influence of cognitive biases. By improving the decision-making process in this way, companies increase the chances that their acquisitions will lead to success rather than to post-merger disaster.

DAN LOVALLO is a professor of management at the University of Western Australia Business School and a senior adviser to McKinsey & Company. **PATRICK VIGUERIE** is a director in McKinsey's Atlanta office. **ROBERT UHLANER** is a partner in the firm's West Coast office. **JOHN HORN** is an associate in the firm's Washington, DC, office.

Originally published in December 2007. Reprint R0712G

Breakthrough Bargaining

by Deborah M. Kolb and Judith Williams

NEGOTIATION WAS ONCE CONSIDERED AN ART practiced by the naturally gifted. To some extent it still is, but increasingly we in the business world have come to regard negotiation as a science—built on creative approaches to deal making that allow everyone to walk away winners of sorts. Executives have become experts at "getting to yes," as the now-familiar terminology goes.

Nevertheless, some negotiations stall or, worse, never get off the ground. Why? Our recent research suggests that the answers lie in a dynamic we have come to call the "shadow negotiation"—the complex and subtle game people play before they get to the table and continue to play after they arrive. The shadow negotiation doesn't determine the "what" of the discussion, but the "how." Which interests will hold sway? Will the conversation's tone be adversarial or cooperative? Whose opinions will be heard? In short, how will bargainers deal with each other?

The shadow negotiation is most obvious when the participants hold unequal power—say, subordinates asking bosses for more resources or new employees engaging with veterans about well-established company policies. Similarly, managers who, because of their race, age, or gender, are in the minority in their companies may be at a disadvantage in the shadow negotiation. Excluded from important networks, they may not have the personal clout, experience, or organizational standing to influence other parties. Even when the bargainers are peers, a negotiation can be blocked or stalled—undermined by hidden assumptions, unrealistic expectations, or personal histories. An unexamined shadow negotiation can lead to silence, not satisfaction.

It doesn't have to be that way. Our research identified strategic levers—we call them power moves, process moves, and appreciative moves—that executives can use to guide the shadow negotiation. In situations in which the other person sees no compelling need to negotiate, *power moves* can help bring him or her to the table. When the dynamics of decision making threaten to overpower a negotiator's voice, *process moves* can reshape the negotiation's structure. And when talks stall because the other party feels pushed or misunderstandings cloud the real issues, *appreciative moves* can alter the tone or atmosphere so that a more collaborative exchange is possible. These strategic moves don't guarantee that bargainers will walk away winners, but they help to get stalled negotiations out of the dark of unspoken power plays and into the light of true dialogue.

Idea in Brief

So much for all those books on "getting to yes." *Your* negotiations keep stalling or, worse, never get off the ground. You can't even get key people to come to the table.

What's going on? It's probably the *shadow negotiation*—unspoken assumptions that determine how bargainers deal with each other, whose opinions get heard, whose interests hold sway. The shadow negotiation looms largest when bargainers hold unequal power—subordinate/boss, new/veteran, male/female, older/younger. *Everyone* struggles with it at some point.

To turn blocked negotiations into constructive dialogue, use these strategic moves.

Power Moves

In the informal negotiations common in the workplace, one of the parties can be operating from a one-down position. The other bargainer, seeing no apparent advantage in negotiating, stalls. Phone calls go unanswered. The meeting keeps being postponed or, if it does take place, a two-way conversation never gets going. Ideas are ignored or overruled, demands dismissed. Such resistance is a natural part of the informal negotiation process. A concern will generally be accorded a fair hearing only when someone believes two things: the other party has something desirable, and one's own objectives will not be met without giving something in return. Willingness to negotiate is, therefore, a confession of mutual need. As a result, a primary objective in the shadow negotiation is fostering the perception of mutual need.

Idea in Practice

POWER MOVES		Offer explicit incentives:	Put a price on inaction:	Enlist support:
To coax reluctant bargainers to participate, show how they'll be better off if they do—and worse off if they don't	EXAMPLES	New executive Fiona Sweeney needed a sweetener to bring together Sales and Production. By improving billing and reducing customer complaints, she demonstrated her value, encouraging both divisions to work with her.	Top performer Karen Hartig's boss wouldn't give her a raise. Exasperated, she got another job offer. He realized the cost of continued inaction, and lobbied for her raise.	Air Force Captain Riley needed consent from a high commander to change flight schedules. He presented a proposal to his immediate superior, who discussed it with the commander. Riley got the commander's blessing.
PROCESS MOVES		Seed ideas early:	Reframe the process:	Build consensus:
When others are making decisions without your input or dismissing your ideas, shape negotiation agendas and dynamics to increase your effectiveness.	EXAMPLES	Joe Lopez turned off peers by overselling his ideas during meetings. When he had one-on-one lunches with colleagues to chat about projects'.	Marcia Philbin lost out to pushier peers in workspace allocations. When she refocused negotiations on corporate concerns, she became chair of a committee	To build consensus on an acquisition, CEO Mark Chapin met individually with key members of both companies, identifying supporters.

	benefits, his peers' receptivity increased.	that developed fair space-allocation criteria.	*and* challengers. He later got supporters to commit before opposers could coalesce.
APPRECIATIVE MOVES	**Help others save face:**	**Keep the dialogue going:**	**Solicit new perspectives:**
Highlight common interests to foster trust and candor—and break stalemates.	EXAMPLES	Sam Newton's boss continually rejected his ideas. Newton realized that his new boss could appear weak if he rubber-stamped proposals. When Newton offered multiple options and acknowledged his boss's authority, their dealings improved.	Software-company development head Fran Rossi met resistance from the research director when she proposed an acquisition. When she gathered more data before drawing him back into the discussions, he reevaluated his position.	HMO executive Donna Hitchcock encountered resistance to implementing an insurance-company joint venture. When she learned that the venture streched her insurance counterpart's overworked departments, they brainstormed ways to alleviate the overload—and implemented the venture.

Power moves can bring reluctant bargainers to the realization that they must negotiate: they will be better off if they do and worse off if they don't. Bargainers can use three kinds of power moves. Incentives emphasize the proposed value to the other person and the advantage to be gained from negotiating. Pressure levers underscore the consequences to the other side if stalling continues. And the third power move, enlisting allies, turns up the volume on the incentives or on the pressure. Here's how these strategies work.

Offer Incentives

In any negotiation, the other party controls something the bargainer needs: money, time, cooperation, communication, and so on. But the bargainer's needs alone aren't enough to bring anyone else to the table. The other side must recognize that benefits will accrue from the negotiation. These benefits must not only be visible— that is, right there on the table—but they must also resonate with the other side's needs. High-tech executive Fiona Sweeney quickly recognized this dynamic when she tried to initiate informal talks about a mission-critical organizational change.

Shortly after being promoted to head operations at an international systems company, Sweeney realized that the organization's decision-making processes required fundamental revamping. The company operated through a collection of fiefdoms, with little coordination even on major accounts. Sales managers, whose bonuses were tied to gross sales, pursued any opportunity with minimal regard for the company's ability to

About the Research

WE BECAME AWARE OF THE SHADOW negotiation as we interviewed, over a five-year period, more than 300 executive women to probe their work experiences in formal and informal negotiations. We spoke with lawyers and bankers, accountants and entrepreneurs, consultants and marketers, project managers and account executives across a range of industries and organizational types. In each interview, we asked about the executive's best and worst negotiation experience. After describing these scenarios, the women wanted to talk with us not only about what worked and why but also about how they might have better handled challenging situations.

During this interviewing and the subsequent writing of *The Shadow Negotiation*, we came to believe that these dialogues and the study's findings have implications for both men and women. The shadow negotiation is where issues of parity, or the equivalence of power, get settled. And parity—its presence or absence—determines to a great extent whether a negotiation takes place at all and on what terms.

---

deliver. Production scrambled to meet unrealistic schedules; budgets and quality suffered. Sweeney had neither the authority nor the inclination to order sales and production to cooperate. And as a newcomer to corporate headquarters, her visibility and credibility were low.

Sweeney needed a sweetener to bring sales and production together. First, she made adjustments to the billing process, reducing errors from 7.1% to 2.4% over a three-month period, thereby cutting back on customer complaints. Almost immediately, her stock shot up with both of the divisions. Second, realizing that sales

The Shadow Campaign

A SINGLE STRATEGIC MOVE SELDOM CARRIES THE DAY. In combination, however, such moves can jump-start workplace negotiations and keep them moving toward resolution.

Consider the case of Fiona Sweeney, the new operations chief introduced earlier in this article. She had neither the authority nor the personal inclination to order the sales and production divisions of her company to cooperate. Instead, she fashioned a series of strategic moves designed to influence the negotiations.

Power Moves

Having established her credibility with sales by increasing the turnaround time on expense-account reimbursements, Sweeney knew she needed to up the ante for maintaining the status quo, which created hardships for production and was frustrating customers. It was particularly important to bring pressure to bear on the sales division, since the informal reward systems, and many of the formal ones, currently worked to its benefit. To disturb the equilibrium, Sweeney began to talk in management meetings about a bonus system that would penalize the sales division whenever it promised more than production could deliver. Rather than immediately acting on this threat, however, she suggested creating a cross-divisional task force to explore the issues. Not surprisingly, sales was eager to be included. Moreover, the CEO let key people know that he backed Sweeney's proposal to base bonuses on profits, not revenues.

Process Moves

Sweeney then moved to exert control over the agenda and build support for the changes she and the CEO envisioned. She started an operations subgroup with the heads of quality control and production, mobilizing allies in the two areas most directly affected by the sales division's behavior. Soon they developed a common agenda and began working in concert to sterm the influence of sales in senior staff meetings. On one occasion, for example, Sweeney proposed assigning a low priority to orders that had not been cleared by the operations subgroup. Quality control and production roundly supported the suggestion, which was soon implemented. Through these process moves, Sweeney built a coalition that shaped the subsequent negotiations. But she did something more.

Power and process moves often provoke resistance from the other side. Sweeney prevented resistance from becoming entrenched within the sales division through a series of appreciative moves.

Appreciative Moves

To deepen her understanding of the issues sales confronted, Sweeney volunteered her operations expertise to the division's planning team. By helping sales develop a new pricing-and-profit model, she not only increased understanding and trust on both sides of the table, but she also paved the way for dialogue on other issues—specifically the need for change in the company's decision-making processes.

Most important, Sweeney never forced any of the players into positions where they would lose face. By using a combination of strategic moves, she helped the sales division realize that change was coming and that it would be better off helping to shape the change than blocking it. In the end, improved communication and cooperation among divisions resulted in increases in both the company's top-line revenues and its profit margins. With better product quality and delivery times, sales actually made more money, and production no longer had the burden of delivering on unrealistic promises generated by sales. Customers—and the CEO—were all happy.

would be more reluctant than production to negotiate any changes in the organization's decision-making processes, she worked with billing to speed up processing the expense-account checks so that salespeople were reimbursed more quickly, a move that immediately got the attention of everyone in sales. By demonstrating her value to sales and production, Sweeney encouraged the two division managers to work with her on improving their joint decision-making process. (For the complete story of Fiona Sweeney's campaign to revamp operations, see the sidebar "The Shadow Campaign.")

Creating value and making it visible are key power moves in the shadow negotiation. A bargainer can't leave it up to the other party to puzzle through the possibilities. The benefits must be made explicit if they are to have any impact on the shadow negotiation. When value disappears, so do influence and bargaining power.

Put a Price on the Status Quo

Abba Eban, Israel's former foreign minister, once observed that diplomats have "a passionate love affair with the status quo" that blocks any forward movement. The same love affair carries over into ordinary negotiations in the workplace. When people believe that a negotiation has the potential to produce bad results for them, they are naturally reluctant to engage on the issues. Until the costs of *not* negotiating are made explicit, ducking the problem will be the easier or safer course.

To unlock the situation, the status quo must be perceived as less attractive. By exerting pressure, the bargainer can raise the cost of business-as-usual until the other side begins to see that things will get worse unless both sides get down to talking.

That is exactly what Karen Hartig, one of the women in our study, did when her boss dragged his heels about giving her a raise. Not only had she been promoted without additional pay, but she was now doing two jobs because the first position had never been filled. Although her boss continued to assure her of his support, nothing changed. Finally, Hartig was so exasperated that she returned a headhunter's call. The resulting job offer provided her with enough leverage to unfreeze the talks with her boss. No longer could he afford to maintain the status quo. By demonstrating that she had another alternative, she gave him the push—and the justification—he needed to argue forcefully on her behalf with his boss and with human resources.

Enlist Support

Solo power moves won't always do the job. Another party may not see sufficient benefits to negotiating, or the potential costs may not be high enough to compel a change of mind. When incentives and pressure levers fail to move the negotiation forward, a bargainer can enlist the help of allies.

Allies are important resources in shadow negotiations. They can be crucial in establishing credibility, and they lend tangible support to incentives already proposed. By providing guidance or running interference, they can favorably position a bargainer's proposals before talks even begin. At a minimum, their confidence primes the other party to listen and raises the costs of not negotiating seriously.

When a member of Dan Riley's squadron faced a prolonged family emergency, the air force captain needed to renegotiate his squadron's flight-rotation orders. The matter was particularly sensitive, however, because it required the consent of the wing commander, two levels up the chain of command. If Riley approached the commander directly, he risked making his immediate superior look bad since his responsibilities covered readiness planning. To bridge that difficulty, Riley presented a draft proposal to his immediate superior. Once aware of the problem, Riley and his superior anticipated some of the objections the commander might raise and then alerted the wing commander to the general difficulties posed by such situations. When Riley finally presented his proposal to the commander, it carried his immediate superior's blessing, and so his credibility was never questioned; only the merits of his solution were discussed.

Process Moves

Rather than attempt to influence the shadow negotiation directly through power moves, a bargainer can exercise another kind of strategic move, the process move. Designed to influence the negotiation process itself, such moves can be particularly effective when bargainers are caught in a dynamic of silencing—when decisions are being made without their input or when colleagues interrupt them during meetings, dismiss their comments, or appropriate their ideas.

While process moves do not address the substantive issues in a negotiation, they directly affect the hearing those issues receive. The agenda, the prenegotiation groundwork, and the sequence in which ideas and people are heard—all these structural elements influence others' receptivity to opinions and demands. Working behind the scenes, a bargainer can plant the seeds of ideas or can marshal support before a position becomes fixed in anyone's mind. Consensus can even be engineered so that the bargainer's agenda frames the subsequent discussion.

Seed Ideas Early

Sometimes parties to a negotiation simply shut down and don't listen; for whatever reason, they screen out particular comments or people. Being ignored in a negotiation doesn't necessarily result from saying too little or saying it too hesitantly. When ideas catch people off guard, they can produce negative, defensive reactions, as can ideas presented too forcefully. Negotiators also screen out the familiar: if they've already heard the speech, or a close variant, they stop paying attention.

Joe Lopez faced this dilemma. Lopez, a fast-track engineer who tended to promote his ideas vigorously in planning meetings, began to notice that his peers were tuning him out—a serious problem since departmental resources were allocated in these sessions. To remedy the situation, Lopez scheduled one-on-one lunch meetings with his colleagues. On each occasion, he mentioned how a particular project would benefit the other manager's department and how they could work together to ensure its completion. As a result of this informal lobbying, Lopez found he no longer needed to oversell his case in the meetings. He could make his ideas heard with fewer words and at a lower decibel level.

Preliminary work like this allows a bargainer to build receptivity where a direct or aggressive approach might encounter resistance. Once the seeds of an idea have been planted, they will influence how others view a situation, regardless of how firmly attached they are to their own beliefs and ideas.

Reframe the Process
Negotiators are not equally adept in all settings. Highly competitive approaches to problem solving favor participants who can bluff and play the game, talk the loudest, hold out the longest, and think fastest on their feet. Bargainers who are uncomfortable with this kind of gamesmanship can reframe the process, shifting the dynamic away from personal competition. That's what Marcia Philbin decided to do about the way in which space was allocated in her company. Extra room and equipment typically went to those who pushed the hardest, and Philbin never fared well in the negotiations. She also believed that significant organizational costs always accompanied the process since group leaders routinely presented the building administrator with inflated figures, making it impossible to assess the company's actual requirements.

Positioning herself as an advocate not only for her department but also for the company, Philbin proposed changing the process. Rather than allocating space in a series of discrete negotiations with the space administrator, she suggested, why not collaborate as a group in developing objective criteria for assessing need? Management agreed, and Philbin soon found herself chairing the committee created to produce the new guidelines. Heated arguments took place over the criteria, but Philbin was now positioned to direct the discussions away from vested and parochial interests toward a greater focus on organizational needs.

Within organizations or groups, negotiations can fall into patterns. If a bargainer's voice is consistently shut out of discussions, something about the way negotiations are structured is working against his or her active participation. A process move may provide a remedy because it will influence how the discussion unfolds and how issues emerge.

Build Consensus

Regardless of how high a bargainer is on the organizational ladder, it is not always possible—or wise—to impose change on a group by fiat. By lobbying behind the scenes, a bargainer can start to build consensus before formal decision making begins. Unlike the first process move, which aims at gaining a hearing for ideas, building consensus creates momentum behind an agenda by bringing others on board. The growing support isolates the blockers, making continued opposition harder and harder. Moreover, once agreement has been secured privately, it becomes difficult (although never impossible) for a supporter to defect publicly.

As CEO of a rapidly growing biotechnology company, Mark Chapin gradually built consensus for his ideas on integrating a newly acquired research boutique into the existing company. Chapin had two goals: to retain the acquired firm's scientific talent and to rationalize the research funding process. The second goal was at odds with the first and threatened to alienate the new scientists. To mitigate this potential conflict, Chapin focused his attention on the shadow negotiation. First, he met one-on-one with key leaders of the board and the research staffs of both companies. These private talks provided him with a strategic map that showed where he would find support and where he was likely to meet challenges. Second, in another round of talks, Chapin paid particular attention to the order in which he approached people. Beginning with the most supportive person, he got the key players to commit, one by one, to his agenda before opposing factions could coalesce. These preliminary meetings positioned him as a collaborator—and, equally important, as a source of expanding research budgets. Having privately built commitment, Chapin found that he didn't need to use his position to dictate terms when the principal players finally sat down to negotiate the integration plan.

Appreciative Moves

Power moves exert influence on the other party so that talks get off the ground. Process moves seek to change the ground rules under which negotiations play out. But still, talks may stall. Two strong advocates may have backed themselves into respective corners. Or one side, put on the defensive, even inadvertently, may continue to resist or raise obstacles. Communication may deteriorate, turn acrimonious, or simply stop as participants focus solely on their own demands. Wariness stifles any candid exchange. And without candor, the two sides cannot address the issues together or uncover the real conflict.

Appreciative moves break these cycles. They explicitly build trust and encourage the other side to participate in a dialogue. Not only do appreciative moves shift the dynamics of the shadow negotiation away from the adversarial, but they also hold out a hidden promise. When bargainers demonstrate appreciation for another's concerns, situation, or "face," they open the negotiation to the different perspectives held by that person and to the opinions, ideas, and feelings shaping those perspectives. Appreciative moves foster open communication so that differences in needs and views can come to the surface without personal discord. Frequently the participants then discover that the problem they were worrying about is not the root conflict, but a symptom of it. And at times, before a negotiation can move toward a common solution, the participants must first experience mutuality, recognizing where their interests and needs intersect. A shared problem can then become the basis for creative problem solving.

Help Others Save Face
Image is a concern for everyone. How negotiators look to themselves and to others who matter to them often

counts as much as the particulars of an agreement. In fact, these are seldom separate. "Face" captures what people value in themselves and the qualities they want others to see in them. Negotiators go to great lengths to preserve face. They stick to their guns against poor odds simply to avoid losing face with those who are counting on them. If a bargainer treads on another's self-image—in front of a boss or colleague, or even privately—his or her demands are likely to be rejected.

Sensitivity to the other side's face does more than head off resistance: it lays the groundwork for trust. It conveys that the bargainer respects what the other is trying to accomplish and will not do anything to embarrass or undermine that person. This appreciation concedes nothing, yet as Sam Newton discovered, it can turn out to be the only way to break a stalemate.

Newton's new boss, transferred from finance, lacked experience on the operations side of the business. During departmental meetings to negotiate project schedules and funding, he always rejected Newton's ideas. Soon it was routine: Newton would make a suggestion and before he got the last sentence out, his boss was issuing a categorical veto.

Frustrated, Newton pushed harder, only to meet increased resistance. Finally, he took a step back and looked at the situation from his boss's perspective. Rubberstamping Newton's proposals could have appeared as a sign of weakness at a time when his boss was still establishing his credentials. From then on, Newton took a different tack. Rather than present a single idea, he offered an array of options and acknowledged that the final decision rested with his boss. Gradually, his boss felt less need to assert his authority and could respond positively in their dealings.

Bosses aren't the only ones who need to save face; colleagues and subordinates do, too. Team members avoid peers who bump a problem upstairs at the first sign of trouble, making everyone appear incapable of producing a solution. Subordinates muzzle their real opinions once they have been belittled or treated dismissively by superiors. In the workplace, attention to face is a show of respect for another person, whatever one's corporate role. That respect carries over to the shadow negotiation.

Keep the Dialogue Going

Sometimes, talks don't get off the ground because the timing is not right for a participant to make a decision; information may be insufficient, or he or she is simply not ready. People have good reasons—at least, reasons that make sense to them—for thinking it's not yet time to negotiate. Appreciating this disposition doesn't mean abandoning or postponing a negotiation. Instead, it requires that a bargainer keep the dialogue going without pushing for immediate agreement. This appreciative move allows an opportunity for additional information to come to the surface and affords the other side more time to rethink ideas and adjust initial predilections.

Francesca Rossi knew instinctively that unless she kept the communication lines open, discussions would derail about the best way for her software firm to grow. The company had recently decided to expand by acquiring promising applications rather than developing them inhouse from scratch. As head of strategic development, Rossi targeted a small start-up that designed state-of-the-art software for office computers to control home appliances. The director of research, however, was less than enthusiastic about acquiring the firm. He questioned the product's commercial viability and argued that its market would never justify the acquisition cost.

Needing his cooperation, Rossi pulled back. Instead of actively promoting the acquisition, she began to work behind the scenes with the start-up's software designers and industry analysts. As Rossi gathered more data in support of the application's potential, she gradually drew the director of research back into the discussions. He dropped his opposition once the analysis convinced him that the acquisition, far from shrinking his department's authority, would actually enlarge it. Rossi's appreciative move had given him the additional information and time he needed to reevaluate his original position.

Not everyone makes decisions quickly. Sometimes people can't see beyond their initial ideas or biases. Given time to mull over the issues, they may eventually reverse course and be more amenable to negotiating. As long as the issue isn't forced or brought to a preemptive conclusion—as long as the participants keep talking— there's a chance that the resistance will fade. What seems unreasonable at one point in a negotiation can become more acceptable at another. Appreciative moves that keep the dialogue going allow the other side to progress at a comfortable speed.

Solicit New Perspectives

One of the biggest barriers to effective negotiation and a major cause of stalemate is the tendency for bargainers to get trapped in their own perspectives. It's simply too easy for people to become overly enamored of their opinions. Operating in a closed world of their making, they tell themselves they are right and the other person is wrong. They consider the merits of their own positions but neglect the other party's valid objections. They push their agendas, merely reiterating the same argument, and may not pick up on cues that their words aren't being heard.

It's safe to assume that the other party is just as convinced that his or her own demands are justified. Moreover, bargainers can only speculate what another's agenda might be—hidden or otherwise. Appreciative moves to draw out another's perspectives help negotiators understand why the other party feels a certain way. But these moves serve more than an instrumental purpose, doing more than add information to a bargainer's arsenal. They signal to the other side that differing opinions and perspectives are important. By creating opportunities to discover something new and unexpected, appreciative moves can break a stalemate. As understanding deepens on both sides of the table, reaching a mutual resolution becomes increasingly possible.

Everyone agreed that a joint venture negotiated by HMO executive Donna Hitchcock between her organization and an insurance company dovetailed with corporate objectives on both sides. The HMO could expand its patient base and the insurance carrier its enrollment.

Although the deal looked good on paper, implementation stalled. Hitchcock couldn't understand where the resistance was coming from or why. In an attempt to unfreeze the situation, she arranged a meeting with her counterpart from the insurance company. After a brief update, Hitchcock asked about any unexpected effects the joint venture was exerting on the insurance carrier's organization and on her counterpart's work life. That appreciative move ultimately broke the logjam. From the carrier's perspective, she learned, the new arrangement stretched already overworked departments and had not yet produced additional revenues to hire more staff. Even more important, her counterpart was personally bearing the burden of the increased work.

Hitchcock was genuinely sympathetic to these concerns. The extra work was a legitimate obstacle to the joint venture's successful implementation. Once she understood the reason behind her counterpart's resistance, the two were able to strategize on ways to alleviate the overload until the additional revenues kicked in.

Through these appreciative moves—actively soliciting the other side's ideas and perspectives, acknowledging their importance, and demonstrating that they are taken seriously—negotiators can encourage the other person to work with them rather than against them.

There's more to negotiation than haggling over issues and working out solutions. The shadow negotiation, though often overlooked, is a critical component. Whether a bargainer uses power, process, or appreciative moves in the shadow negotiation depends on the demands of the situation. Power moves encourage another party to recognize the need to negotiate in the first place. They help bring a reluctant bargainer to the table. Process moves create a context in which a bargainer can shape the negotiation's agenda and dynamic so that he or she can be a more effective advocate. Appreciative moves engage the other party in a collaborative exchange by fostering trust and candor in the shadow negotiation. While power and process moves can ensure that a negotiation gets started on the right foot, appreciative moves can break a stalemate once a negotiation is underway. By broadening the discourse, appreciative moves can also lead to creative solutions. Used alone or in combination, strategic moves in the shadow negotiation can determine the outcome of the negotiation on the issues.

Note

1. Most of the negotiating stories used in this article have been adapted from *The Shadow Negotiation: How Women Can Master the Hidden Agendas That Determine Bargaining Success* (Simon & Schuster, 2000) and the authors' interviews with businesspeople. To respect interviewees' candor and to protect their privacy, their identities and situations have been disguised, sometimes radically.

DEBORAH M. KOLB is a professor of management at the Simmons School of Management in Boston and codirector of its Center for Gender in Organizations. **JUDITH WILLIAMS** is the founder of Anagram, a nonprofit corporation dedicated to the study of social and organizational change.

Originally published in February 2001. Reprint 6080

Building Deals on Bedrock

by David Harding and Sam Rovit

WHETHER THEY LIKE IT or not, most CEOs recognize that their companies can't succeed without making acquisitions. It has become virtually impossible, in fact, to create a world-class company through organic growth alone. Most industries grow at a relatively slow pace, but investors expect companies to grow quickly. Not everyone can steal market share, particularly in mature industries. Sooner or later, companies must turn to acquisitions to help fill the gap.

Yet acquisitions can be a treacherous way to grow. In their bids for new opportunities, many companies lose sight of the fundamental rules for making money in their industries. Look at what happened to manufacturing giant Newell.

When Newell's top managers approached their counterparts at Rubbermaid in 1999 about the possibility of a merger, it looked like a deal from heaven. Newell had a 30-year track record of building shareholder value through successful acquisitions of companies like

Levolor, Calphalon, and Sanford, maker of Sharpie pens. Rubbermaid had recently topped *Fortune*'s list of the most admired U.S. companies and was a true blue-chip firm. With its long record of innovation, it was very profitable and growing quickly.

Because Newell and Rubbermaid both sold household products through essentially the same sales channels, the cost synergies from the combination loomed large. Newell expected to reap the benefits of Rubbermaid's high-margin branded products—a range of low-tech plastic items, from laundry baskets to Little Tikes toys—while fixing a number of weak links in its supply chain.

Rubbermaid's executives were encouraging: As long as the deal could be done quickly, they said, they'd give Newell an exclusive right to acquire their company. Eager to seize the opportunity, Newell rushed to close the $5.8 billion megamerger—a deal ten times larger than any it had done before.

But the deal from heaven turned out, to use *BusinessWeek*'s phrase, to be the "merger from hell." Instead of lifting Newell to a new level of growth, the acquisition dragged the company down. In 2002, Newell wrote off $500 million in goodwill, leading its former CEO and chairman, Daniel Ferguson, to admit, "We paid too much." By that time, Newell shareholders had lost 50% of the value of their investment; Rubbermaid shareholders had lost 35%.

What went wrong? It's tempting to brush off the failure as a lack of due diligence or an error in execution. Admittedly, when Newell looked beneath Rubbermaid's

Idea in Brief

The headlines are filled with the sorry tales of companies like Vivendi and AOL Time Warner that tried to use mergers and acquisitions to grow big fast or transform fundamentally weak business models. But, drawing on extensive data and experience, the authors conclude that major deals make sense in only two circumstances: when they reinforce a company's existing basis of competition or when they help a company make the shift, as the industry's competitive base changes. In most stable industries, the authors contend, only one basis—superior cost position, brand power, consumer loyalty, real-asset advantage, or government protection—leads to industry leadership, and companies should do only those deals that bolster a strategy to capitalize on that competitive base. That's what Kellogg did when it acquired Keebler. Rather than bow to price pressures from lesser players, Kellogg sought to strengthen its existing basis of competition—

its brand—through Keebler's innovative distribution system. A company coping with a changing industry should embark on a series of acquisitions (most likely coupled with divestitures) aimed at moving the firm to the new competitive basis. That's what Comcast did when changes in government regulations fundamentally altered the broadcast industry. In such cases, speed is essential, the investments required are huge, and half measures can be worse than nothing at all. Still, the research shows that successful acquirers are not those that try to swallow a single, large, supposedly transformative deal but those that go to the M&A table often and take small bites. Deals can fuel growth—as long as they're anchored in the fundamental way money is made in your industry. Fail to understand that and no amount of integration planning will keep you and your shareholders from bearing the high cost of your mistakes.

well-polished exterior after the deal closed, it discovered a raft of problems, from extensive price discounting for wholesalers to poor customer service to weak management. And Newell's management team, accustomed to integrating small "tuck in" deals, greatly underestimated the challenge of choreographing a merger of equals.

Yet even without those problems, Newell would have run into difficulties. That's because the deal was flawed from the start. Although Rubbermaid and Newell both sold household basics to the same pool of customers, the two companies had fundamentally different bases of competition. Levolor blinds and Calphalon pots notwithstanding, Newell competed primarily by efficiently churning out prosaic goods that could be sold at cut-rate prices. Rubbermaid was a classic brand company. Even though its products were low-tech, they sold at premium prices because they were distinctive and innovative. Rubbermaid could afford to pay less attention to operating efficiency. The two companies had different production processes and cost structures; they used different value propositions to appeal to customers. If Newell's executives had remained focused on the company's own basis of competition—being a low-cost producer—they would have seen from the outset that Rubbermaid was incompatible.

How can acquirers avoid the Rubbermaid trap? We've been studying the question for years. In fact, we've analyzed 15 years' worth of data (from 1986 through 2001) from more than 1,700 companies in the United States, Europe, and Japan; interviewed 250 CEOs in depth; and worked with dozens of big companies in planning and implementing mergers and acquisitions. Our research has confirmed our experience, leading us to conclude that major deals make sense in only two circumstances: when they buttress a company's current basis of competition or when they enable a company to lead or keep up with its industry as it shifts to a different basis of competition. In other words, the primary purpose of mergers and acquisitions is not to grow big fast, although that may be the result, but for companies to do what they do better.

That means some companies should never do major deals. Firms that have a truly unique competitive edge— the Nikes, Southwests, Enterprise Rent-A-Cars, and Dells of the world—should avoid big deals altogether. For such companies, large-scale acquisitions are usually counterproductive, diluting their unique advantages and hampering future growth.

It also follows that the odds are overwhelmingly against the success of a single headline-grabbing megadeal. If you already do what you do better than anyone else, a big merger or acquisition can only siphon money, resources, time, and management attention away from the core business. And even if you don't, rarely will a single deal be the solution to all your company's problems and bring no issues of its own.

Perhaps this sounds self-evident. But few companies are so strategic in their approach to mergers and acquisitions. When we surveyed 250 senior executives who had done major deals, more than 40% said they had no investment thesis—meaning they had no theory of how the deal would boost profits and stock price. And half of those who did have an investment thesis discovered within three years of closing the deal that their approach was wrong. That means fewer than one in three executives went into deals with a sound reason that actually stood the test of time for buying a company. All too many of them made the same mistake Newell did with Rubbermaid: pursuing an acquisition that conflicted fundamentally with their company's existing or desired basis of competition.

In this article, we'll examine how successful acquirers in both stable and changing industries use the basis of competition to guide their deal-making decisions. We'll also explore how a company's rigorous understanding of its basis of competition can change the way it approaches the deal-making process. But first, let's take a closer look at what we mean by basis of competition.

The Basis of Competition

Much of the allure in the notion that acquisitions enable companies to get big fast must lie in its connection with a related idea: that industry leadership equals market share leadership. That is, the leading companies in an industry are those with the most customers and the highest sales. But if this were true, American Airlines would be far more successful than Southwest, IBM would still be the industry leader in computer hardware, and Hertz would be more profitable than Enterprise.

If size is no necessary virtue in a particular industry, then virtue must lie elsewhere. In our experience, what determines industry leadership varies significantly from field to field. We propose that, broadly speaking, companies can achieve industry leadership in five

---

The finer points of competitive advantage

The basis for competition differs by industry, and wise acquirers know their basis before they launch a deal.

Basis	Companies
Superior cost position	Newell, Wal-Mart
Brand power	Procter & Gamble, Kellogg
Customer loyalty	Enterprise Rent-A-Car, MBNA
Real-asset advantage	Harrods, IMC Global
Government protection	GlaxoSmithKline, Comcast

---

ways: through superior cost position, brand power, consumer loyalty, real-asset advantage, and government protection. (See the exhibit "The finer points of competitive advantage.") Getting bigger may bolster one or more of these bases of competition, but it doesn't guarantee leadership. And recognizing which basis matters the most in a given industry can be tricky.

For instance, what's the basis of competition for the venerable British department store Harrods? While the company's name is certainly well known, its brand is not the main reason the trendy shop can sustain its high margins. And even though its upscale British service is important, customer loyalty is not the primary basis of competition either. Rather, it's the shop's premier address in London's tony Knightsbridge neighborhood—an asset advantage—that allows Harrods to charge the high prices it does.

On what basis does independent credit card issuer MBNA compete? It's not just that its size confers economies of scale. In the financial services industry, cost-to-income ratios determine the winners. The cost of acquiring new customers is so substantial that the highest returns go to the companies that capture the largest share of wallet from their best customers. In short, MBNA and companies like it compete on customer loyalty. Accordingly, MBNA's strategy focuses on bolstering customer retention by getting the right customers, not just getting the most customers. That approach guided its acquisition in 2004 of Sky Financial Solutions, a company that provides financing for dental professionals. With nearly three-quarters of all dentists in the United States already carrying an MBNA credit card, the Sky deal offered a way for MBNA to cement loyalty and expand its share of wallet.

And what about Comcast? It excels at managing blue-collar contractors and negotiating with content providers, but it does not compete primarily through asset advantage. Its monthly billing system is highly efficient, but it does not compete primarily on cost either. Competing in a regulated industry, its primary advantage lies in being a master of red tape: obtaining rights of way and negotiating with local municipalities to assure rates. So it competes primarily on the basis of government protection.

One of the things that makes recognizing a company's basis of competition less than straightforward is that few organizations are pure play. Low-cost producer Newell, you may recall, also had some strong brands. Yet as a manufacturer, its cost position is what tends to seal its fate. Conversely, while Rubbermaid was a manufacturer, as with most consumer products companies, its earnings capacity was primarily tied to its brand power.

When firms do deals that strengthen their basis of competition, as MBNA did, they increase their earning power; when they don't, they weaken their earning power. Clearly, then, every merger or acquisition your company proposes to do—whether big or small, strategic or tactical—should start with a clear statement of how money is made in your business (what the company's basis of competition is) and how adding this particular acquisition to your portfolio will further your strategy for capitalizing on that basis and thereby make the firm more valuable. If this were easy, far more acquisitions would succeed. Let's take a look at how one company used those principles to guide its acquisitions and grow profitability in an industry whose basis of competition was stable—although at first glance it may not have seemed that way.

Building on Success

Every multinational food company with sales greater than $5 billion grew through extensive acquisitions. It's not hard to see why. New products are essential for growth, and it's cheaper to buy a new sandwich spread or snack food than to develop one. Merger and acquisition activity in this industry has been especially intense during the past ten years, which have seen a host of acquisitions by the large food companies: Philip Morris's Kraft buying Nabisco, General Mills purchasing Pillsbury, Sara Lee gobbling up Earthgrains, to name only a few. One of the most successful acquisitions was Kellogg's takeover of Keebler, a good example of a company that knew what it was buying and why and that reaped the returns to prove it.

Kellogg's basis of competition is unquestionably its brand strength. For decades, a shelf full of household-name products like Corn Flakes, Rice Krispies, and Special K steadily delivered top-tier operating margins of 17.5% and a leading share of the ready-to-eat cereal market. The company's strong brand meant it could raise prices just enough each year to generate the upside profit surprises that shareholders love.

But by the mid-1990s, Kellogg's once-crisp universe was growing soggy. Post, the number three competitor, had initiated a fierce price war. General Mills, the traditional number two, began vying for market share lead. Retailers stepped up offerings of store brands, with companies like Ralston Foods happily supplying these goods at lower prices. Worse still, to more and more consumers, that bowl of Corn Flakes, once considered the obligatory way to start the day, was becoming a hassle in a time-constrained world. Between 1996 and 2000, Kellogg's share price dropped nearly 20% in a booming stock market.

This was the situation Carlos Gutierrez inherited when he became the company's CEO in 1999. Despite the cost pressures from Post, Gutierrez and his team recognized that Kellogg's brand strength, not its cost position, remained its strongest competitive weapon. Even if people were skipping breakfast, they still liked to snack on cereal-based products during the day.

Between 1996 and 2001, the market for handheld breakfast bars grew 8% annually even as demand for ready-
to-eat cereals declined 5% year after year. Kellogg had
strong brands that lent themselves well to snacking, notably its Nutri-Grain bars and Rice Krispies Treats.

Firmly committed to *what* the company did—
compete on brand—Gutierrez and his team focused on
how they could do it better, paying particular attention
to the capabilities Kellogg would need to sustain its
brand strength in a rapidly consolidating marketplace.
They concluded that the company had to excel in three
areas: new-product development, broader distribution,
and the creation of a culture skilled at executing business plans more quickly.

Revamping Kellogg's culture and creating new products could be addressed internally by training people
differently and by redirecting spending on capital and
R&D projects. Distribution, however, was another matter. The best way to deliver snacks was through a direct
distribution channel. But building one from scratch
would be inordinately expensive. Kellogg needed to
buy one.

Gutierrez and his team set their sights on Illinois-
based Keebler. Keebler was the number two cookie and
cracker maker in the United States, behind Nabisco. But
it wasn't Keebler's cookie-making prowess that excited
Kellogg; it was where Keebler sold its cookies and how it
got them there. Keebler had an outstanding direct
store-delivery system. Rather than ship products to a
retailer's warehouse and expect the retailer to put them
on the shelves, Keebler sent out a fleet of panel trucks

every day to deliver fresh snacks directly from its bakeries to store aisles, greatly speeding inventory turns.

Kellogg calculated that acquiring Keebler would add one to two points to the top line by moving Kellogg into a high-growth distribution channel and by filling that channel with an expanded line of snacks. The Keebler acquisition became pivotal in Kellogg's turnaround, as revenue rose 43% between 1999 and 2003 and operating income nearly doubled. The key to the deal's success was that it allowed the company to extend its existing brand strength into new products and additional channels.

Kellogg's decision to build its brand even as the very concept of breakfast was changing might appear risky. In our experience, however, company leaders consistently underestimate the potential left in their core businesses. High-performing companies drive their businesses to achieve full market share and profit potential before taking on something new.

That's a lesson IMC Global learned—eventually. For many years, IMC was the leading North American producer of phosphates and the number two producer of potash, two key ingredients in crop fertilizer. During the late 1990s, IMC tried to extend its traditional basis of competition—asset advantage—by bolstering its phosphate and potash mines and processing plants with a move into specialty chemicals. But what looked like a push into a related business was not. The specialty chemicals business had different supply chains and customers from those of the phosphate- and potash-mining business. What's more, the phosphate industry was still highly fragmented, and IMC over-looked the opportunity to roll up companies in its core business. The businesses IMC bought did not enhance its asset advantage, either by growing its share of potash and phosphate assets, or by adding new technology to lower its costs, or by bringing in new points of distribution. Instead, the acquisitions added leverage to the balance sheet and diverted management time and cash from maintaining IMC's leadership position in its core fertilizer business.

A new management team brought in to turn around the business recognized that future growth and profitability hinged on restoring the focus on phosphates and widening distribution in what had become a global market. The new team divested all the businesses unrelated to fertilizers that had been added during the late 1990s. In early 2004, IMC agreed to merge with $2 billion Cargill Crop Nutrition, a move that increased its phosphate mining and processing capacity. And in a market where all the growth is coming from less-developed countries, Cargill Crop Nutrition's global distribution system provides a source of competitive advantage for Mosaic, the new company. Though the deal is still in its early stages, preliminary results are good, and we expect it to be successful in the long run because the deal is squarely in line with the way IMC makes its money.

Using Deals to Power Change

At the other end of the spectrum from the IMC and Cargill scenario are the glamorous, high-profile deals aimed at transforming companies or entire industries. The idea of using acquisitions as strategic master-strokes gained momentum throughout the 1990s, and a host of high-flying companies, including Vivendi Universal, AOL Time Warner (which changed its name back to Time Warner in October 2003), Enron, and natural gas provider Williams employed the technique.

That list alone may be enough to turn readers off to the concept. But the approach shouldn't be discarded entirely, because when the basis of competition in an industry changes, transformational deals can make sense. Advances in technology, shifts in regulations, and the emergence of new competitors can change an industry's competitive base so abruptly that even the fastest organizations can't alter their core businesses rapidly enough to adapt organically to the new market, leaving acquisitions as the best way to recast the business. Much, however, hangs in the balance. Speed is critical, the investments required are enormous, and taking half measures can be worse than doing nothing at all.

Getting it right requires companies to have a clear understanding of the new basis of competition, and one big deal seldom offers the best way to get there. Clear Channel Communications is one company that successfully used a series of deals to segue to stronger growth, after the foundation for competition in its industry shifted dramatically in the 1990s. Let's see how.

Lowry Mays was an accidental radio entrepreneur. The former investment banker found himself in the radio business when a friend backed out of a radio station deal in 1972, and Mays was left holding the property. During the next 23 years, Mays and his two sons became accomplished deal makers in broadcasting, acquiring two dozen radio stations one by one, most for less than $40 million. Government regulation formed the basis of competition in radio broadcasting during the 1970s and 1980s, and success lay in securing exclusive licenses granted by the Federal Communications Commission in particular local markets.

Knowing what their business was about, the Mayses were clever in how they built it. They were savvy financiers, bolstering cash flow from radio operations with debt financing to fund expansion. They became expert at anticipating when local radio stations were about to come up for sale. When those stations hit the market, the Mayses were prepared with strong bids.

Using this approach, the Mayses' company, Clear Channel, vaulted to number six in radio broadcast revenues, close behind Infinity Broadcasting, Evergreen Media, Disney, Chancellor Broadcasting, and Cox Broadcasting. By 1995, however, the Mayses had hit a ceiling. Federal law limited broadcasters to two stations per market and 40 nationwide, and Clear Channel was bumping up against those barriers. Then the game changed. In 1996, Congress deregulated the industry, allowing companies to own as many as eight stations in a large market and eliminating nationwide limits entirely. Overnight, the basis of competition in radio shifted. Cost leadership would determine the industry's winners rather than skill in trading up to the most lucrative local licenses. The Mayses understood that this new basis of competition favored operating on a national and possibly a global scale, which would enable broadcasters to spread their costs.

Players in the radio broadcasting industry divided into two camps: the buyers and the bought. The Mayses intended to be buyers. As the industry redefined itself, Clear Channel applied a savvy strategy to this new basis of competition. It combined aggressive acquisitions to gain scale with innovative new operating practices—such as providing packaged playlists, centrally distributing formats to stations around the country, and using the same "local" weatherman to report on cities as distant from each other as Tampa and San Diego—to capitalize on its size.

Clear Channel's coherent strategy quickly moved it to the top of the industry. At the beginning of 2004, the company owned about 1,200 radio stations in the United States and had equity interests in more than 240 stations internationally. Its next nearest competitor, Viacom, owned about one-fifth as many stations.

Clear Channel's steady focus on cost led the company to look beyond broadcasting as well. In 1997, it spotted cross selling and bundling opportunities for local advertising and diversified into the billboard business by acquiring a succession of small companies. Then, in 2000, it became the leading live-concert promoter through the acquisition of SFX Entertainment.

The financial results of Clear Channel's acquisition-driven growth strategy have been exceptional, as each deal has reinforced the company's shift to cost-based competition. From 1995 through 2003, company revenues and income grew at an astounding rate of 55% annually. Clear Channel generated a 28% average annual shareholder return during the same period.

While Clear Channel was able to adjust to the realities of a changing industry through a series of acquisitions, most firms moving to a new basis of competition will almost certainly need to consider divestitures as well. Otherwise, they will find themselves trying to compete in two different ways—a sure recipe for failure. An example of an effective acquirer-divestor is the Thomson Corporation. From 1997 to 2002, Thomson transformed itself from a traditional conglomerate that included newspapers, travel services, and professional publications into a focused provider of integrated electronic information to specialty markets. This made sense, as the growth of the Internet had changed the basis of competition in its industry from customer loyalty (newspaper subscriptions and renewals) into real-asset advantage (ownership of proprietary databases).

Starting in 1997, Thomson zeroed in on a small number of businesses in its portfolio that were especially well positioned to capitalize on the industry's shift. As Thomson's executives saw it, the new basis of competition centered on achieving scale by developing proprietary technologies that transformed the way information was delivered and integrated into the workplace. Exploiting this technological potential became the core of the Thomson investment thesis. Thomson realized that continuing to use its newspapers as a way to distribute information that originated with wire services owned by others would become an indefensible position, as the

Internet made alternate modes of publication much cheaper and easier. Instead, it needed to own the information, so it divested newspapers and bought databases. Thomson sold more than 60 companies and 130 newspapers, raising $6 billion. With the proceeds, it invested heavily in its core markets by acquiring more than 200 businesses in educational, legal, tax, accounting, scientific, health care, and financial information publishing. Over the course of this transformation, the company improved its operating margin by 6%. Today, Thomson is a leader in electronic information databases; owning the information allows the company to earn superior returns.

Disciplining the Deal

Adopting such a strategic approach to M&A argues for an equally deliberate approach to managing the M&A process within your company. Yet the most common approach could hardly be called deliberate, much less strategic. Here's what usually happens.

An investment banker calls up the CEO with a target for sale and a deal book that provides background material. "This is your chance to be the industry leader," he declares. Or maybe he says, "Your core business is stagnant; you need to look elsewhere for growth."

In response, the corporate development staffers run off and do a quick screen, based on a cursory review of the book and a superficial industry overview. If they discover that the banker is bending the truth or that the company in question is in a lot of trouble, they balk. But

Slow and steady

Our research shows that continual acquirers that make small deals consistently earn higher returns than those that do fewer and larger deals.

Number of deals

Average annual excess returns

Number of deals made by U.S. acquirers (1986–2001)

| 94 | 228 | 155 | 79 | 58 | 33 | 27 | 50 |

Number of firms

Relative size of deals

Average annual excess returns

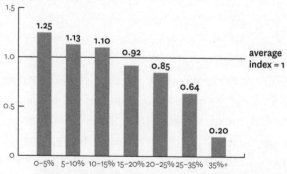

Average transaction value as a percentage of market cap (U.S. acquirers, 1986–2001)

| 173 | 201 | 69 | 33 | 17 | 29 | 33 |

Number of firms

Source: Bain & Company Global Learning Curve study (2002–2003)

if the deal still looks "interesting"—however that may be defined—they construct a valuation model and conduct financial and legal due diligence.

In a few weeks, the team builds a case for the deal. Then they dive into hundreds of hours of negotiations, presentations, and board discussions—all aimed more or less consciously at naming a price that will fly and getting a green light from the board.

We hope none of this sounds familiar to you, because the odds are stacked high against picking a deal successfully this way. If the acquisition team is reacting rather than acting, it's likely to pursue plain vanilla deals with prices below the valuation model, deals with limited upside and almost unlimited downside. Meanwhile, the team will turn down deals that appear to be too expensive but actually aren't in terms of their long-term strategic benefits. And it will fail to uncover opportunities it might turn up on its own if it followed a strategic road map.

The best acquirers follow a process we call "planning for opportunity." Long before any opportunity arises, these people have their basis of competition firmly in mind, and the strategy they need to capitalize on it is carefully considered. They think long and hard about what kinds of deals they should be pursuing. Then a corporate M&A team works with individuals who are closer to the ground in the line organizations to create a pipeline of priority targets, each with a customized investment thesis, and together, they look for opportunities to win over interesting prospects. They systematically cultivate a relationship with each target so that they are positioned to get to the table as soon as (or, even better, before) the target goes on sale. By this stage, canny acquirers are likely to have months or even years invested in the prospective deal. As a result, they're often willing to pay a premium or act more quickly than rivals because they know precisely what they can expect to achieve through the acquisition.

Thus, seasoned acquirer Cintas, a leading manufacturer of uniforms in the United States and Canada, assigns someone to keep in touch with each potential target, often for years. This individual, who comes from the line organization, reports to the corporate M&A team, which ensures that she stays in touch with the target and watches for favorable conditions to pull the trigger on talks. Indeed, the deal team sometimes even "puts a bullet in the gun" by giving senior executives a compelling reason to contact the target if changes in that company, or in the marketplace, warrant it. Through this sophisticated system, the $2.7 billion Cincinnati-based company has sustained its sales growth for 34 years at a compound annual rate of 23%. Profits have grown at an even more impressive 30% annually.

By now it should be clear that strategic deal making generally argues against the big-bang approach of transforming a business through a massive acquisition. Our analysis of the deals made by 1,700 acquirers between 1986 and 2001 underscores the fact that the most successful acquirers do a lot of deals, that they do deals more or less continually, and that the average deal size is small. In our database, U.S. companies that did

20 deals or more during the 15-year period generated shareholder returns almost twice as high as the returns from companies that did no deals at all. Frequent acquirers outperformed those that did fewer than five deals by a factor of 1.7. And companies that acquired firms for 15% or less of the value of their own market capitalization on average earned returns six times higher than those that bought companies 35% of their size or larger. (See the exhibit "Slow and steady.") The conclusion is clear: Go to the table frequently, and take small bites.

Can deal making solve your growth problem? In many cases, yes, as long as those deals are built on a sound competitive foundation and anchored in the fundamental way your company makes money. Understand that, and you've taken the first step toward M&A success. Fail to take that step, and no amount of integration planning will keep you and your shareholders from bearing the high cost of your mistakes.

DAVID HARDING is a director in Bain & Company's Boston office and a leader in the firm's strategy and organization practices. **SAM ROVIT** is a Bain director based in Chicago and leads the firm's global mergers and acquisitions practice. They are the authors of *Mastering the Merger: Four Critical Decisions That Make or Break the Deal* (Harvard Business Review Press, 2004).

Originally published in September 2004. Reprint R0409J

Getting Past Yes

Negotiating as if Implementation Mattered

by Danny Ertel

IN JULY 1998, AT&T AND BT announced a new 50/50 joint venture that promised to bring global interconnectivity to multinational customers. Concert, as the venture was called, was launched with great fanfare and even greater expectations: The $10 billion start-up would pool assets, talent, and relationships and was expected to log $1 billion in profits from day one. Just three years later, Concert was out of business. It had laid off 2,300 employees, announced $7 billion in charges, and returned its infrastructure assets to the parent companies. To be sure, the weak market played a role in Concert's demise, but the way the deal was put together certainly hammered a few nails into the coffin.

For example, AT&T's deal makers scored what they probably considered a valuable win when they negotiated a way for AT&T Solutions to retain key multinational customers for itself. As a result, AT&T and BT ended up in direct competition for business—exactly what the Concert venture was supposed to help prevent. For its part, BT seemingly outnegotiated AT&T by refusing to contribute to AT&T's purchase of the IBM Global Network. That move saved BT money, but it muddied Concert's strategy, leaving the start-up to contend with overlapping products. In 2000, Concert announced a complex new arrangement that was supposed to clarify its strategy, but many questions about account ownership, revenue recognition, and competing offerings went unanswered. Ultimately, the two parent companies pulled the plug on the venture.[1]

Concert is hardly the only alliance that began with a signed contract and a champagne toast but ended in bitter disappointment. Examples abound of deals that look terrific on paper but never materialize into effective, value-creating endeavors. And it's not just alliances that can go bad during implementation. Misfortune can befall a whole range of agreements that involve two or more parties—mergers, acquisitions, outsourcing contracts, even internal projects that require the cooperation of more than one department. Although the problem often masquerades as one of execution, its roots are anchored in the deal's inception, when negotiators act as if their main objective were to sign the deal. To be successful, negotiators must recognize that signing a contract is just the beginning of the process of creating value.

During the past 20 years, I've analyzed or assisted in hundreds of complex negotiations, both through my research at the Harvard Negotiation Project and through my consulting practice. And I've seen countless deals that were signed with optimism fall apart during implementation, despite the care and creativity with which their terms were crafted. The crux of the problem is that the

Idea in Brief

Why do so many deals that looked great on paper end up in tatters? Negotiators on both sides probably focused too much on closing the deals and squeezing the best terms out of one another—and not enough on implementation. Bargainers with this **deal maker mind-set** never ask how—or whether—their agreement will work *in practice*. Once implementation begins, surprises and disappointments crop up—often torpedoing the deal.

How to avoid this scenario? Bargain using an **implementation mind-set**. Define negotiation not as closing the deal but as setting the stage for a successful long-term relationship. Brainstorm and discuss problems you might encounter

12 months down the road. Help the other party think through the agreement's practical implications, so your counterparts won't promise something they can't deliver. Ensure that both sides' stakeholders support the deal. And communicate a consistent message about the deal's terms and spirit to both parties' implementation teams.

Deals negotiated from an implementation mind-set don't "sizzle" like those struck by bargainers practicing brinksmanship. But as companies like HP Services and Procter & Gamble have discovered, a deal's real value comes not from a signature on a document but from the real work performed long after the ink has dried.

very person everyone thinks is central to the deal—the negotiator—is often the one who undermines the partnership's ability to succeed. The real challenge lies not in hammering out little victories on the way to signing on the dotted line but in designing a deal that works in practice.

The Danger of Deal Makers

It's easy to see where the deal maker mind-set comes from. The media glorifies big-name deal makers like Donald Trump, Michael Ovitz, and Bruce Wasserstein.

Idea in Practice

To adopt an implementation mind-set, apply these practices *before* inking a deal:

Start with the End in Mind

Imagine that it's a year into implementation of your deal. Ask:

- **Is the deal working?** What metrics are you using to measure its success?

- **What has gone wrong so far?** What have you done to put things back on course? What signals suggest trouble ahead?

- **What capabilities are needed to accomplish the deal's objectives?** What skills do your implementation teams need? Who has tried to block implementation, and how have you responded?

By answering these questions now, you avoid being blindsided by surprises during implementation.

Help the Other Party Prepare

Coming to the table prepared to negotiate a workable deal isn't enough—your *counterpart* must also prepare. Before negotiations begin, encourage the other party to consult with their internal stakeholders throughout the bargaining process. Explain who you think the key players are, who should be involved early on, and what key questions about implementation you're asking yourself.

Treat Alignment as a Shared Responsibility

Jointly address how you'll build broad support for the deal's implementation. Identify both parties' stakeholders—those who will make decisions, affect the deal's success through

Books like *You Can Negotiate Anything, Trump: The Art of the Deal,* and even my own partners' *Getting to Yes* all position the end of the negotiation as the destination. And most companies evaluate and compensate negotiators based on the size of the deals they're signing.

But what kind of behavior does this approach create? People who view the contract as the conclusion and see themselves as solely responsible for getting there action or inaction, hold critical budgets, or possess crucial information. Map how and when different stakeholders' input will be solicited. Ask who needs to know what in order to support the deal and carry out their part of its implementation.

Send One Message

Ensure that each team responsible for implementing the deal understands what the agreement is meant to accomplish. Communicate *one* message to them about the terms of the deal, the spirit in which it was negotiated, and the trade-offs that were made to craft the final contract.

Example: During IBM Global Services' "joint handoff meetings," the company's negotiators and their counterparts brief implementation teams on what's in the contract, what's different or nonstandard, and what the deal's ultimate intent is.

Manage Negotiation Like a Business Process

Establish a disciplined process for negotiation preparation in your company. Provide training in collaborative negotiation tools and techniques for negotiators *and* implementers. Use post-negotiation reviews to capture learning. And reward individuals for the delivered success of the deals they negotiated—not for how those deals look on paper.

behave very differently from those who see the agreement as just the beginning and believe their role is to ensure that the parties involved actually realize the value they are trying to create. These two camps have conflicting opinions about the use of surprise and the sharing of information. They also differ in how much attention they pay to whether the parties' commitments are realistic, whether their stakeholders are sufficiently aligned,

Deal-minded negotiators

versus

Implementation-minded negotiators

Negotiation Tactics

= Surprise =

= Information sharing =

Deal-minded negotiators

Assumption
"Surprising them helps me. They may commit to something they might not have otherwise, and we'll get a better deal."

Behaviors
Introduce new actors or information at strategic points in negotiation.

Raise new issues at the end.

Assumption
"It's not my role to equip them with relevant information or to correct their misperceptions."

Behaviors
Withhold information.

Fail to correct mistaken impressions.

Implementation-minded negotiators

Assumption
"Surprising them puts us at risk. They may commit to something they cannot deliver or will regret."

Behaviors
Propose agendas in advance so both parties can prepare.

Suggest questions to be discussed, and provide relevant data.

Raise issues early.

Assumption
"I don't want them entering this deal feeling duped. I want their goodwill during implementation, not their grudging compliance."

Behaviors
Create a joint fact-gathering group.

Commission third-party research and analysis.

Question everyone's assumptions openly.

	Closing techniques	
Assumption "My job is to get the deal closed. It's worth putting a little pressure on them now and coping with their unhappiness later." **Behaviors** Create artificial deadlines. Threaten escalation. Make "this day only" offers.	=	**Assumption** "My job is to create value by crafting a workable agreement. Investing a little extra time in making sure both sides are aligned is worth the effort." **Behaviors** Define interests that need to be considered for the deal to be successful. Define joint communication strategy.

	Realistic commitments	
Assumptions "As long as they commit, that's all that matters. Afterward, it's their problem if they don't deliver." **Behaviors** Focus on documenting commitments rather than on testing the practicality of those commitments. Rely on penalty clauses for protection.	=	**Assumption** "If they fail to deliver, we don't get the value we expect." **Behaviors** Ask tough questions about both parties' ability to deliver. Make implementability a shared concern. Establish early warning systems and contingency plans.

	Decision making and stakeholders	
Assumption "The fewer people involved in making this decision, the better and faster this will go." **Behaviors** Limit participation in discussions to decision makers. Keep outsiders in the dark until it is too late for them to derail things.	=	**Assumption** "If we both fail to involve key stakeholders sufficiently and early enough, whatever time we save now will be lost during implementation." **Behaviors** Repeatedly ask about stakeholders: Whose approval is needed? Whose cooperation is required? Who might interfere with implementation?

and whether those who must implement the deal can establish a suitable working relationship with one another. (For a comparison of how different mind-sets affect negotiation behaviors, see the exhibit "Deal-minded negotiators versus implementation-minded negotiators.")

This isn't to say deal makers are sleazy, dishonest, or unethical. Being a deal maker means being a good closer. The deal maker mind-set is the ideal approach in certain circumstances. For example, when negotiating the sale of an asset in which title will simply be transferred and the parties will have little or no need to work together, getting the signatures on the page really does define success.

But frequently a signed contract represents a commitment to work together to create value. When that's the case, the manner in which the parties "get to yes" matters a great deal. Unfortunately, many organizations structure their negotiation teams and manage the flow of information in ways that actually hurt a deal's chances of being implemented well.

An organization that embraces the deal maker approach, for instance, tends to structure its business development teams in a way that drives an ever growing stream of new deals. These dedicated teams, responsible for keeping negotiations on track and getting deals done, build tactical expertise, acquire knowledge of useful contract terms, and go on to sign more deals. But they also become detached from implementation and are likely to focus more on the agreement than on its business impact. Just think about the language deal-making teams use ("closing" a deal, putting a deal "to bed") and how their performance is measured and rewarded (in terms of the number and size of deals closed and the time required to close them). These teams want to sign a piece of paper and book the expected value; they couldn't care less about launching a relationship.

The much talked about Business Affairs engine at AOL under David Colburn is one extreme example. The group became so focused on doing deals—the larger and more lopsided the better—that it lost sight of the need to have its business partners actually remain in business or to have its deals produce more than paper value. In 2002, following internal investigations and probes by the SEC and the Department of Justice, AOL Time Warner concluded it needed to restate financial results to account for the real value (or lack thereof) created by some of those deals.[2]

The deal maker mentality also fosters the take-no-prisoners attitude common in procurement organizations. The aim: Squeeze your counterpart for the best possible deal you can get. Instead of focusing on deal volume, as business development engines do, these groups concentrate on how many concessions they can get. The desire to win outweighs the costs of signing a deal that cannot work in practice because the supplier will never be able to make enough money.

Think about how companies handle negotiations with outsourcing providers. Few organizations contract out enough of their work to have as much expertise as the providers themselves in negotiating deal structures, terms and conditions, metrics, pricing, and the like, so they frequently engage a third-party adviser to help level

A New Mind-Set

FIVE APPROACHES CAN HELP your negotiating team transition from a deal maker mentality to an implementation mind-set.

1. **Start with the end in mind.** Imagine the deal 12 months out: What has gone wrong? How do you know if it's a success? Who should have been involved earlier?

2. **Help them prepare, too.** Surprising the other side doesn't make sense, because if they promise things they can't deliver, you both lose.

3. **Treat alignment as a shared responsibility.** If your counterpart's interests aren't aligned, it's your problem, too.

4. **Send one message.** Brief implementation teams on both sides of the deal together so everyone has the same information.

5. **Manage negotiation like a business process.** Combine a disciplined preparation process with postnegotiation reviews.

---

the playing field as they select an outsourcer and hammer out a contract. Some advisers actually trumpet their role in commoditizing the providers' solutions so they can create "apples to apples" comparison charts, engender competitive bidding, and drive down prices. To maximize competitive tension, they exert tight control, blocking virtually all communications between would-be customers and service providers. That means the outsourcers have almost no opportunity to design solutions tailored to the customer's unique business drivers.

The results are fairly predictable. The deal structure that both customer and provider teams are left to implement is the one that was easiest to compare with other bids, not the one that would have created the most value. Worse yet, when the negotiators on each side exit the process, the people responsible for making the deal work are virtual strangers and lack a nuanced understanding of why issues were handled the way they were. Furthermore, neither side has earned the trust of its partner during negotiations. The hard feelings created by the hired guns can linger for years.

The fact is, organizations that depend on negotiations for growth can't afford to abdicate management responsibility for the process. It would be foolhardy to leave negotiations entirely up to the individual wits and skills of those sitting at the table on any given day. That's why some corporations have taken steps to make negotiation an organizational competence. They have made the process more structured by, for instance, applying Six Sigma discipline or community of practice principles to improve outcomes and learn from past experiences.

Sarbanes-Oxley and an emphasis on greater management accountability will only reinforce this trend. As more companies (and their auditors) recognize the need to move to a controls-based approach for their deal-making processes—be they in sales, sourcing, or business development—they will need to implement metrics, tools, and process disciplines that preserve creativity and let managers truly manage negotiators. How they do so, and how they define the role of the negotiator, will determine whether deals end up creating or destroying value.

Negotiating for Implementation

Making the leap to an implementation mind-set requires five shifts.

1. Start with the end in mind

For the involved parties to reap the benefits outlined in the agreement, goodwill and collaboration are needed during implementation. That's why negotiation teams should carry out a simple "benefit of hindsight" exercise as part of their preparation.

Imagine that it is 12 months into the deal, and ask yourself:

> *Is the deal working?* What metrics are we using? If quantitative metrics are too hard to define, what other indications of success can we use?

> *What has gone wrong so far?* What have we done to put things back on course? What were some early warning signals that the deal may not meet its objectives?

> *What capabilities are necessary to accomplish our objectives?* What processes and tools must be in place? What skills must the implementation teams have? What attitudes or assumptions are required of those who must implement the deal? Who has tried to block implementation, and how have we responded?

If negotiators are required to answer those kinds of questions before the deal is finalized, they cannot help but behave differently. For example, if the negotiators of the Concert joint venture had followed that line of questioning before closing the deal, they might have asked themselves, "What good is winning the right to keep customers out of the deal if doing so leads to competition between the alliance's parents? And if we have to take that risk, can we put in mechanisms now to help mitigate it?" Raising those tough questions probably wouldn't have made a negotiator popular, but it might have led to different terms in the deal and certainly to different processes and metrics in the implementation plan.

Most organizations with experience in negotiating complex deals know that some terms have a tendency to come back and bite them during implementation. For example, in 50/50 ventures, the partner with greater leverage often secures the right to break ties if the new venture's steering committee should ever come to an impasse on an issue. In practice, though, that means executives from the dominant party who go into negotiations to resolve such impasses don't really have to engage with the other side. At the end of the day, they know they can simply impose their decision. But when that happens, the relationship is frequently broken beyond repair.

Tom Finn, vice president of strategic planning and alliances at Procter & Gamble Pharmaceuticals, has made it his mission to incorporate tough lessons like that into the negotiation process itself. Although Finn's alliance management responsibilities technically don't start until after a deal has been negotiated by the P&G Pharmaceuticals business development organization, Finn jumps into the negotiation process to ensure negotiators do not bargain for terms that will cause trouble down the road. "It's not just a matter of a win-win philosophy," he says. "It's about incorporating our alliance managers' hard-won experience with terms that cause implementation problems and not letting those terms into our deals."

Finn and his team avoid things like step-down royalties and unequal profit splits with 50/50 expense sharing, to name just a few. "It's important that the partners be provided [with] incentives to do the right thing," Finn says. "When those incentives shift, you tend to end up [with] difficulties." Step-down royalties, for instance, are a common structure in the industry. They're predicated on the assumption that a brand is made or lost in the first three years, so that thereafter, payments to the originator should go down. But P&G Pharmaceuticals believes it is important to provide incentives to the partner to continue to work hard over time. As for concerns about overpaying for the licensed compound in the latter years of the contract, Finn asserts that "leaving some money on the table is OK if you realize that the most expensive deal is one that fails."

2. Help them prepare, too

If implementation is the name of the game, then coming to the table well prepared is necessary—but not sufficient. Your counterpart must also be prepared to negotiate a workable deal. Some negotiators believe they can gain advantage by surprising the other side. But surprise confers advantage only because the counterpart has failed to think through all the implications of a proposal and might mistakenly commit to something it wouldn't have if it had been better prepared. While that kind of an advantage might pay off in a simple buy-sell transaction, it fails miserably—for both sides—in any situation that requires a long-term working relationship.

That's why it's in your best interest to engage with your counterpart before negotiations start. Encourage the other party to do its homework and consult with its internal stakeholders before and throughout the negotiation process. Let the team know who you think the key players are, who should be involved early on, how you hope to build implementation planning into the negotiation process, and what key questions you are asking yourself.

Take the example of Equitas, a major reinsurer in the London market. When preparing for commutations negotiations—whereby two reinsurers settle their mutual book of business—the company sends its counterpart a thorough kickoff package, which is used as the agenda for the negotiation launch meeting. This "commutations action pack" describes how the reinsurer's own commutations department is organized, what its preferred approach to a commutations negotiation is, and what stages it follows. It also includes a suggested approach to policy reconciliation and due diligence and explains what data the reinsurer has available—even acknowledging its imperfections and gaps. The package describes critical issues for the reinsurer and provides sample agreements and memorandums for various stages of the process.

The kickoff meeting thus offers a structured environment in which the parties can educate each other on their decision-making processes and their expectations for the deal. The language of the commutations action pack and the collaborative spirit of the kickoff meeting are designed to help the parties get to know each other and settle on a way of working together before they start making the difficult trade-offs that will be required of them. By establishing an agreed-upon process for how and when to communicate with brokers about the deal, the two sides are better able to manage the tension between the need to include stakeholders who are critical to implementation and the need to maintain confidentiality before the deal is signed.

Aventis Pharma is another example of how measured disclosure of background and other information can pave the way to smoother negotiations and stronger implementation. Like many of its peers, the British pharmaceutical giant wants potential biotech partners to see it as a partner of choice and value a relationship with the company for more than the size of the royalty check involved. To that end, Aventis has developed and piloted a "negotiation launch" process, which it describes as a meeting during which parties about to enter into formal negotiations plan together for those negotiations. Such collaboration allows both sides to identify potential issues and set up an agreed upon process and time line. The company asserts that while "formally launching negotiations with a counterpart may seem unorthodox to some," the entire negotiation process runs more efficiently and effectively when partners "take the time to discuss how they will negotiate before beginning."

3. Treat alignment as a shared responsibility
If their interests are not aligned, and they cannot deliver fully, that's not just their problem—it's your problem, too.

Unfortunately, deal makers often rely on secrecy to achieve their goals (after all, a stakeholder who doesn't know about a deal can't object). But leaving internal stakeholders in the dark about a potential deal can have negative consequences. Individuals and departments that will be directly affected don't have a chance to weigh in with suggestions to mitigate risks or improve the outcome. And people with relevant information about the deal don't share it, because they have no idea it's needed. Instead, the typical reaction managers have when confronted late in the game with news of a deal that will affect their department is "Not with my FTEs, you don't."

Turning a blind eye to likely alignment problems on the other side of the table is one of the leading reasons alliances break down and one of the major sources of conflict in outsourcing deals. Many companies, for instance, have outsourced some of their human resource or finance and accounting processes. Service providers, for their part, often move labor-intensive processes to Web-based self-service systems to gain process efficiencies. If users find the new self-service system frustrating or intimidating, though, they make repeated (and expensive) calls to service centers or fax in handwritten forms. As a result, processing costs jump from pennies per transaction to tens of dollars per transaction.

But during the initial negotiation, buyers routinely fail to disclose just how undisciplined their processes are and how resistant to change their cultures might be. After all, they think, those problems will be the provider's headache once the deal is signed. Meanwhile, to make requested price concessions, providers often drop line items from their proposals intended to educate employees and support the new process. In exchange for such concessions, with a wink and a nod, negotiators assure the provider that the buyers will dedicate internal resources to change-management and communication efforts. No one asks whether business unit managers support the deal or whether function leaders are prepared to make the transition from managing the actual work to managing the relationship with an external provider. Everyone simply agrees, the deal is signed, and the frustration begins.

As managers and employees work around the new self-service system, the provider's costs increase, the service levels fall (because the provider was not staffed for the high level of calls and faxes), and customer satisfaction plummets. Finger-pointing ensues, which must then be addressed through expensive additions to the contract, costly modifications to processes and technology, and additional burdens on a communication and change effort already laden with baggage from the initial failure.

Building alignment is among negotiators' least favorite activities. The deal makers often feel as if they are wasting precious time "negotiating internally" instead of working their magic on the other side. But without acceptance of the deal by those who are essential to its implementation (or who can place obstacles in the way), proceeding with the deal is even more wasteful. Alignment is a classic "pay me now or pay me later" problem. To understand whether the deal will work in practice, the negotiation process must encompass not only subject matter experts or those with bargaining authority but also those who will actually have to take critical actions or refrain from pursuing conflicting avenues later.

Because significant deals often require both parties to preserve some degree of confidentiality, the matter of involving the right stakeholders at the right time is more effectively addressed jointly than unilaterally. With an understanding of who the different stakeholders are—including those who have necessary information, those who hold critical budgets, those who manage important third-party relationships, and so on—a joint communications subteam can then map how, when, and with whom different inputs will be solicited and different categories of information might be shared. For example, some stakeholders may need to know that the negotiations are taking place but not the identity of the counterpart. Others may need only to be aware that the organization is seeking to form a partnership so they can prepare for the potential effects of an eventual deal. And while some must remain in the dark, suitable proxies should be identified to ensure that their perspectives (and the roles they will play during implementation) are considered at the table.

4. Send one message
Complex deals require the participation of many people during implementation, so once the agreement is in place, it's essential that the team that created it get

everyone up to speed on the terms of the deal, on the mind-set under which it was negotiated, and on the trade-offs that were made in crafting the final contract. When each implementation team is given the contract in a vacuum and then is left to interpret it separately, each develops a different picture of what the deal is meant to accomplish, of the negotiators' intentions, and of what wasn't actually written in the document but each had imagined would be true in practice.

"If your objective is to have a deal you can implement, then you want the actual people who will be there, after the negotiators move on, up front and listening to the dialogue and the give-and-take during the negotiation so they understand how you got to the agreed solution," says Steve Fenn, vice president for retail industry and former VP for global business development at IBM Global Services. "But we can't always have the delivery executive at the table, and our customer doesn't always know who from their side is going to be around to lead the relationship." To address this challenge, Fenn uses joint hand-off meetings, at which he and his counterpart brief both sides of the delivery equation. "We tell them what's in the contract, what is different or nonstandard, what the schedules cover. But more important, we clarify the intent of the deal: Here's what we had difficulty with, and here's what we ended up with and why. We don't try to reinterpret the language of the contract but [we do try] to discuss openly the spirit of the contract." These meetings are usually attended by the individual who developed the statement of work, the person who priced the deal, the contracts and negotiation lead, and occasionally legal counsel. This team briefs the project executive in charge of the implementation effort and the executive's direct reports. Participation on the customer side varies, because the early days in an outsourcing relationship are often hectic and full of turnover. But Fenn works with the project executive and the sales team to identify the key customer representatives who should be invited to the hand-off briefing.

Negotiators who know they have to brief the implementation team with their counterparts after the deal is signed will approach the entire negotiation differently. They'll start asking the sort of tough questions at the negotiating table that they imagine they'll have to field during the postdeal briefings. And as they think about how they will explain the deal to the delivery team, they will begin to marshal defensible precedents, norms, industry practices, and objective criteria. Such standards of legitimacy strengthen the relationship because they emphasize persuasion rather than coercion. Ultimately, this practice makes a deal more viable because attention shifts from the individual negotiators and their personalities toward the merits of the arrangement.

5. Manage negotiation like a business process

Negotiating as if implementation mattered isn't a simple task. You must worry about the costs and challenges of execution rather than just getting the other side to say yes. You must carry out all the internal consultations necessary to build alignment. And you must make sure your counterparts are as prepared as you are. Each of these actions can feel like a big time sink. Deal makers don't want to spend time negotiating with their own people to build alignment or risk having their counterparts pull out once they know all the details. If a company wants its negotiators to sign deals that create real value, though, it has to weed out that deal maker mentality from its ranks. Fortunately, it can be done with simple processes and controls. (For an example of how HP Services structures its negotiation process, see the sidebar "Negotiating Credibility.")

More and more outsourcing and procurement firms are adopting a disciplined negotiation preparation process. Some even require a manager to review the output of that process before authorizing the negotiator to proceed with the deal. KLA-Tencor, a semiconductor production equipment maker, uses the electronic tools available through its supplier-management Web site for this purpose, for example. Its managers can capture valuable information about negotiators' practices, including the issues they are coming up against, the options they are proposing, the standards of legitimacy they are relying on, and the walkaway alternatives they are considering. Coupled with simple postnegotiation reviews, this information can yield powerful organizational insights.

Preparing for successful implementation is hard work, and it has a lot less sizzle than the brinksmanship characteristic of the negotiation process itself. To overcome the natural tendency to ignore feasibility questions, it's important for management to send a clear message about the value of postdeal implementation. It must reward individuals, at least in part, based on the delivered success of the deals they negotiate, not on how those deals look on paper. This practice is fairly standard among outsourcing service providers; it's one that should be adopted more broadly.

Improving the implementability of deals is not just about layering controls or capturing data. After all, a manager's strength has much to do with the skills she chooses to build and reward and the example she sets with her own questions and actions. In the health care arena, where payer-provider contentions are legion, forward-thinking payers and innovative providers are among those trying to change the dynamics of deals and develop agreements that work better. Blue Cross and Blue Shield of Florida, for example, has been working to institutionalize an approach to payer-provider negotiations that strengthens the working relationship and supports implementation. Training in collaborative negotiation tools and techniques has been rolled down from the senior executives to the negotiators to the support and analysis teams. Even more important, those who manage relationships with providers and are responsible for implementing the agreements are given the same training and tools. In other words, the entire process of putting the deal together, making it work, and feeding the lessons learned through implementation back into the negotiation process has been tightly integrated.

Most competitive runners will tell you that if you train to get to the finish line, you will lose the race. To win, you have to envision your goal as just beyond the finish

Negotiating Credibility

HP SERVICES IS GROWING in a highly competitive market, and its success is partly due to its approach to negotiating large outsourcing transactions. In a maturing market, where top tier providers can demonstrate comparable capabilities and where price variations inevitably diminish after companies bid against one another time and time again, a provider's ability to manage a relationship and build trust are key differentiators. The negotiation and the set of interactions leading up to it give the customer a first taste of what it will be like to solve problems with the provider during the life of the contract. "Decisions made by clients regarding selection have as much to do with the company they want to do business with as with price, capability, and reliability," acknowledges Steve Huhn, HP Services' vice president of strategic outsourcing. "Negotiating these kinds of deals requires being honest, open, and credible. Integrity is critical to our credibility."

Huhn's team of negotiators uses a well-structured process designed to make sure that the philosophy of integrity is pervasive throughout the negotiation and not just a function of who happens to be at the table on any given day. It begins with the formation of a negotiation team. Because transition in complex outsourcing transactions represents a period of high vulnerability, it is important to involve implementation staff early on; that way, any commitments made can be validated by those who will be responsible for keeping them. A typical negotiation team consists of a business leader, or pursuit lead, who is usually responsible for developing the business and structuring the transaction; a contract specialist, who brings

line so you will blow right past it at full speed. The same is true for a negotiator: If signing the document is your ultimate goal, you will fall short of a winning deal.

The product of a negotiation isn't a document; it's the value produced once the parties have done what experience with outsourcing contract terms and conditions; and the proposed client manager, who will be responsible for delivery.

Negotiation leads work with a high degree of autonomy. Huhn believes that a negotiator without authority is little more than a messenger, and messengers are unlikely to earn trust or build working relationships with counterparts. At HP, negotiators earn that autonomy by preparing extensively with templates and by reviewing key deal parameters with management. A negotiator's mandate does not just cover price: It also encompasses margins, cash flow, and ROI at different times in the life of the contract; the treatment of transferred employees; the ways various kinds of risk will be allocated; and how the relationship will be governed. All these interests must be addressed—both in preparation and at the negotiation table.

HP's outsourcing negotiators are subject to informal reviews with full-time deal coaches as well as formal milestone reviews. The reviews, which are designed to get key stakeholders committed to implementation, happen before the formal proposal is delivered and before the deal is signed.

The pursuit team leaders aren't finished once the agreement is signed. In fact, they retain responsibility during the transition phase and are considered "liable" for the deal's performance during the next 18 to 24 months. That means negotiators can't simply jump to the next alluring deal. On the contrary, they have a vested interest in making sure the closed deal actually meets its targets.

they agreed to do. Negotiators who understand that prepare differently than deal makers do. They don't ask, "What might they be willing to accept?" but rather, "How do we create value together?" They also negotiate differently, recognizing that value comes not from a signature but from real work performed long after the ink has dried.

Notes

1. For more perspectives on Concert's demise, see Margie Semilof's 2001 article "Concert Plays Its Last Note" on InternetWeek.com; Brian Washburn's 2000 article "Disconcerted" on Tele.com; and Charles Hodson's 2001 article "Concert: What Went Wrong?" on CNN.com.

2. See Alec Klein, "Lord of the Flies," the *Washington Post,* June 15, 2003, and Gary Rivlin, "AOL's Rough Riders," *Industry Standard,* October 30, 2000, for more information on the AOL Business Affairs department's practices.

DANNY ERTEL is the CEO of Vantage Technologies, which develops software to enable negotiation and relationship management processes.

Originally published in November 2004. Reprint R0411C

Negotiating without a Net

A Conversation with the NYPD's
Dominick J. Misino

Diane L. Coutu

NEGOTIATION INFORMS ALL ASPECTS of business life. Every interaction—with customers, with suppliers, and even with partners and investors—involves some kind of negotiation. In fact, in some languages the same term is used for both "business" and "negotiation." But the costs of failure can be high. The breakdown of negotiations between Hewlett-Packard's management and its founding families, for example, put the company's future in doubt and led to an expensive proxy fight.

Perhaps it's not surprising, then, that the last 20 years have seen an endless stream of handbooks on business negotiation, many of them best-sellers. Or that most of the country's top business schools have entire academic departments devoted to the subject. The advice is often helpful, even insightful. Who could argue with the recommendation that negotiators look for mutual gain and know their best alternative to a negotiated agreement?

But you can't help feeling that the scholarly ink and classroom simulations of Negotiation 101 don't do enough to prepare businesspeople for the really tough negotiations—the ones where failure is not an option.

So where can you look for guidance? For the last three decades, the New York Police Department has been training officers in hostage negotiation, arguably the highest-stake situation of all. Founded in 1972, in the year after the Attica State Prison riot, the NYPD program was the country's first such training program. Another year later, in the wake of the Munich Olympics hostage crisis, the FBI established its own program, which was modeled on the NYPD's. Today, most law enforcement agencies in this country and others provide some kind of negotiation training, as local and national law enforcement officials face bargaining with armed criminals, terrorists, and psychopaths as part of their daily reality.

To find out what businesspeople can learn about handling tough negotiations from the experience of law enforcement, HBR senior editor Diane L. Coutu visited former NYPD detective and hostage negotiator Dominick Misino at his home on Long Island, New York (where he can be reached at negotiate1@aol.com). A member of the force for 22 years, Misino received international acclaim in 1993 when he successfully persuaded the hijacker of Lufthansa Flight 592 to lay down his gun and turn himself in at Kennedy Airport. Misino spent the last six years of his career as a primary negotiator, handling more than 200 incidents and never losing a single life.

Since retiring in 1995, he has taught negotiating skills to law enforcement officials, military personnel, and

Idea in Brief

In some languages, the word for "business" is the same as the word for "negotiation." That's not really surprising: Every interaction—with customers, suppliers, and even partners and investors—entails negotiation. And some involve very high stakes: The breakdown in negotiations between Hewlett-Packard's management and its founding families, for instance, put the company's future in doubt. Dominick Misino is a man who knows about negotiating when the stakes are at their very highest. As a hostage negotiator for the New York Police Department, Misino successfully persuaded the hijacker of Lufthansa Flight 592 to lay down his gun and turn himself in. Misino spent the last 6 years of his career as a primary negotiator, handling more than 200 incidents and never losing a life. Since his retirement in 1995, he has taught negotiating skills to law enforcement officials, military personnel, and business executives. Negotiation, he says, is really a series of small agreements, and he is adept at orchestrating those agreements from the start so that his adversary learns to trust him and come around to his point of view. In vivid and sometimes hair-raising detail, Misino demonstrates how he gets criminals to trust police officers enough to refrain from harming innocent parties and give themselves up. Many of the techniques he describes are surprisingly applicable to business negotiations, where the parties may seem equally intractable and failure is not an option.

business executives (for more details, see his Web site, hostagenegotiation.com). Misino modestly describes hostage negotiation as "applied common sense." In the following interview, edited for clarity and length, he explores what he means by that innocuous-sounding term, painting a vivid picture of the blood, sweat, and tears of hostage negotiation.

What special skills does it take to be a crisis negotiator?

I don't think it requires special skills. Anyone can do it, man or woman, uniformed or civilian. What crisis negotiation does take is what I call applied common sense. When I'm negotiating, I'm constantly asking myself, "What is the simplest thing I can do to solve the problem?" When I'm dealing with an armed criminal, for example, my first rule of thumb is simply to be polite. This sounds trite, I know, but it is very important.

A lot of times, the people I'm dealing with are extremely nasty. And the reason for this is that their anxiety level is so high: A guy armed and barricaded in a bank is in a fight-or-flight mode. To defuse the situation, I've got to try to understand what's going on in his head. The first step to getting there is to show him respect, which shows my sincerity and reliability. So before the bad guy demands anything, I always ask him if he needs something. Obviously I'm not going to get him a car. I'm not going to let him go. But it makes excellent sense to be sensitive to the other guy's needs. When you give somebody a little something, he feels obligated to give you something back. That's just good common sense.

Don't you find it difficult to be polite to a murderer or a rapist?

I'll go even further. How do you show respect to a convicted child molester? Believe me, in my line of work we routinely deal with people who have moved out of society and done things that are just horrific. Obviously, it isn't easy to negotiate with someone you dislike—but if you're a professional you keep your feelings separate from your work.

In crisis negotiation, you have the advantage that your goal is constantly right in front of your face: Get everybody out alive. And you're also under incredible time pressure. When an Ethiopian national hijacked that Lufthansa plane, I had less than 45 minutes to build a relationship with him and bring the plane down. There were 104 people on board, and the hijacker had a gun aimed at the pilot's head. That's all the motivation I needed to stay focused on my task. Of course, there are people—whole countries, even—who say that we should never negotiate with certain individuals—terrorists, for instance. But I think that's extreme. In reality, we're always ready to negotiate as hard as we can with anyone to show him that there is an alternative to violence. Of course, we're also ready to come in with a tactical solution—to deploy the SWAT teams—if we have to. But, ideally, force is a last resort.

Can you give other examples of what you mean by applied common sense?

Another very commonsense technique is to ask the bad guy very early on in a negotiation if he wants you to tell him the truth. I stumbled on this tactic when I first started negotiating. My backup team found out that the bad guy had been part of a street gang. So I said, "Look, you grew up on the streets. So did I. Do you want me to lie to you or tell the truth?" And he said he wanted the truth, which, of course, is exactly what I expected him to say. His situation was desperate; there were snipers all over the place. Who in his right mind would have wanted to be lied to?

The critical thing you get by asking the other guy if he wants the truth is that he enters into an agreement with you right at the start. This is important because a successful negotiation is really a series of small agree-ments. You use every possible opportunity to agree with your adversary—and to get him to agree with you. Because all the while you're agreeing, the other guy is learning that he can trust you, that nobody's going to hurt him. So I try right away to get to the first yes, and then immediately I go for the second. I tell the bad guy that if he wants me to tell him the truth, then he might hear things he doesn't want to hear and, if that hap-pens, he's got to agree not to hurt anybody. In my day, I've negotiated with hostage-takers, hijackers, and murderers; the majority of them have given me their word they won't hurt anyone. These people may be the outcasts of society, but they do have a code of honor. In fact, I would say that over 90% of the times that a crim-inal has given me his promise, he has kept it.

If you don't have to learn special skills, do you need certain personal qualities to be a successful high-stakes negotiator?

On the most basic level, you have to be a good lis-tener. Unfortunately, like most people, negotiators want to talk and be heard, and so they've got to learn how to let the other person express himself without interrup-tion. That's terribly important because the individuals with whom we are dealing are often the very people who have never been listened to, and they are desperate to be heard. They just don't have the patience for you to butt in and make a mistake. To get around this, I try to be a very active listener. For example, I typically ask the other guy to tell me his side of things. And then I sit back and get an earful. I hear every instance of when the other guy has ever been wronged. I find out how often he's been framed. I discover how no one has ever cared for him. And a lot of this is true. But the way I look at it is that all of it is true—to him. And that's what matters.

So top negotiators are excellent listeners. But they also need to be aware of the noise inside their own heads. Believe me, even if you don't know what's going on inside you, the other guy will. Their sensitivity to your own biases is extraordinary. You need to know your hot buttons and your limitations.

Personally, I've got a lot of trouble dealing with ped-erasts and other people who harm children. But never-theless I can negotiate with these people because I'm aware of my feelings. I would even say my feelings push me to become a better negotiator because when I know that something is going to affect me, I work harder to achieve a level of objectivity. That's all part of being com-fortable with who you are, which is essential for being able to negotiate. Take police negotiations: They are im-promptu and can go on for 50 minutes or ten hours; no-body knows. The only thing for certain is that no one can sustain a facade under that kind of pressure for very long. So the best preparation in the world for a successful negotiation is just to be comfortable with yourself.

Your reference to active listening sounds very reminiscent of what psychoanalysts call empathic listening. Can you say more?

Almost by definition, crisis negotiation is a roller coaster of emotions, both yours and the other guy's. To me, active listening means being attuned to those emotions, identifying them, and helping the other guy to work them through. One of the most effective ways of doing this is by a technique we call mirroring. We echo the other guy's remarks to try and build a bridge between us. For example, I'll say, "So, you have a gun."

And typically the bad guy says, "Yeah, I have a gun."

"A gun?" I repeat.

"Yeah," he says, "a nine-millimeter gun."

And so I echo him again: "nine-millimeter?"

"Yeah, nine-millimeter with two magazines, 18 rounds."

In this exchange, of course, I'm getting critical data. But at the same time I'm telling the bad guy that there is no longer a gun separating him and me; instead, there is some vital piece of information that the two of us share. In this way, mirroring is the beginning of a real conversation.

Another active-listening technique is to be constantly on the alert for the feelings being expressed behind the words. This is not as obvious as it sounds. My former partner once had an elderly woman who had barricaded herself in a house with a ten-inch butcher knife, and she was cursing at him at the top of her lungs. Despite her profanity, my partner was able to detect something else. He said to her, "Martha, I can hear your pain. I hear it in your voice." And she went from ranting and raving to absolute silence. No one before had ever picked up on the fact that she was hurting so much. When my partner acknowledged her pain, she put down the butcher knife, and he could begin to treat her like the elderly grandmother she was.

It sounds hokey until you've experienced it, but the very act of listening is empathetic. And when we do talk, we try to reinforce the empathy by using a lot of "we" statements: "We're in this together" or "We can work this out." This is the kind of language that can alleviate the bad guy's isolation and paranoia.

It sounds as if you're trying to put yourself in the other guy's shoes. Is that right?

Up to a point, but you've got to be careful about telling a hijacker or a rapist that you know exactly what he's going through, because usually you don't. In fact, you can really infuriate people by trying to identify with them, because they know that you know very little about what they've been through in their lives. One time, one of our guys tried to commiserate with a bad guy, and the guy just went ballistic. He started cursing and screaming: "When was the last time *you* ever held up a bank and took five hostages?" So putting yourself in the other guy's shoes isn't always as helpful as it sounds. In fact, I've often been struck in my own negotiations by how impossible it is for me to imagine the amount of stress a bad guy feels when he's holed up in a building with 100 heavily armed SWAT team officers focused on him, watching his every move. Truthfully, I have probably never felt as scared or angry or lonely in my entire life as that guy does at that moment.

You've talked about good negotiators; what makes a bad one?

The worst negotiators are the people who hate rejection. Of course, nobody likes rejection—it hurts your feelings. But bad negotiators can't accept the fact that all the negative stuff coming at them is not personal. They think the other guy is angry at them when the other guy doesn't even know them. I used to get yelled at all the time in my job, but as I tell my students, you just have to let the other person vent. Because if you do, there's an incredible payoff.

First of all, the other guy usually feels better. But even more important, in the process of letting off steam, the bad guy is likely to tell you his problem—and the solution to his problem. For instance, I once heard a bad guy ranting and raving because a negotiator was Italian. That helped us figure out pretty quickly that the negotiator had to go. But generally speaking, bad negotiators lack this perspective. They get their feelings hurt, which makes them soft—or defensive. Both are bad positions from which to negotiate.

So the other guy needs to vent. What about you?

Certainly you experience a lot of negative emotions in this job. You feel rage and frustration; you are almost always scared. I once participated in a negotiation that went on for 12 hours, though I wasn't the prime negotiator all that time. The most frustrating part was that the guy refused to talk. He just wouldn't talk. I have a tape recording of the negotiation, and whenever I hear it again, I realize how totally pent up I was feeling. I think if I could have reached out and strangled that guy, I probably would have.

There's nothing wrong with having strong emotions during a negotiation, but you need to acknowledge them so you don't act them out. That's the rule of thumb. But even here there are some exceptions. The most aggressive thing I've ever said in a negotiation situation was to a burglar who was threatening to kill his hostage, an 84-year-old lady named Ruth. As his threats grew more intense, I felt rage coming up inside me. And I said to the guy, "If you touch a hair on her head, I will personally ID your body in the morgue." Now, threatening your hostage-taker is not a suggested negotiation tactic. But in this situation, my gut told me that if I sat there all day listening to this particular guy threaten this particular lady, he was going to kill her. So I had to intervene. I did, and instantly the criminal backed down.

That was the only time I ever threatened a criminal in this way, but at the same time I must admit that I do not believe the best negotiators *never* act on their feelings. I think if you don't find yourself taking some risks in this job—if you don't find yourself going someplace you never intended on going—then you probably aren't being the best negotiator you can be.

It seems that you have to put a lid on some strong feelings. What helps you do that?

Having a team behind you is essential. Back in the early days, there were no negotiation teams. Negotiators worked one-on-one, and the stress was extraordinary. The longest consecutive negotiation I ever did was nine hours, and that was like running the New York City marathon. I just can't imagine how anyone could survive an ordeal like that without team support.

Nowadays, most police negotiation teams consist of five people. There is the primary negotiator, who actually talks to the bad guy. Then there is the commander, who makes all the decisions, and the coach who provides moral support and backup. These are the primary players. There's also a gopher or float, who runs around gathering vital information, and a guy we call a scribe. He keeps a chronological log of all the important stuff that's going on during the negotiation. It sounds crazy, but one of the things you often forget in the heat of a hostage situation is the other guy's name. So the scribe writes that down in big black letters on a piece of paper, which he tapes to the wall of the house or apartment we're negotiating out of.

An important point about these teams is that they're deliberately set up to separate negotiation from decision making, which gives the primary negotiator both terrific relief and enormous power to negotiate. Imagine for a moment that you're negotiating, and you tell the bad guy that you're in charge. He responds by demanding a car in 30 minutes or he'll take out a hostage. If, on the other hand, you can say, "Look, my commander is in charge, and I have to consult him," you've bought yourself time to maneuver.

This is the way diplomats operate all the time. They work out a proposal and then bring it back to the national leaders for approval. Of course, in a crisis situation you don't have days and months to discuss a proposal. You don't even have minutes. You come to a fork in the road, and you have fractions of seconds to decide whether to go right or left. This kind of pressure would be unendurable without a team's direction.

I guess that a lot of the time you didn't meet the people you were dealing with face-to-face. Was that a problem?

I hate to say it, but face-to-face communication is very old-fashioned. We rarely do that nowadays. Originally, the NYPD agreed with the communication gurus who said that face-to-face negotiation creates more intimacy and trust. But we quickly found out that face-to-face communication with a psychopath or an armed criminal is highly dangerous. In fact, the only police negotiators who have ever been killed in a negotiation situation were those who had face-to-face contact. So we dropped the approach altogether except for those situations in which there is absolutely no other way.

Normally, we prefer to work with the other guy by phone. Either we tap a phone line or drop a phone into the barricaded zone. However we manage it, phone contact is extremely effective. Americans are totally comfortable with the phone. We argue on the phone; we drive and talk on the phone; I've even heard of people who do therapy on the phone. Ironically, in my experience, the bad guys are often more comfortable on the phone than in face-to-face contact because they feel safer being at some distance from the police. If they're standing in the same room with you, they feel more exposed.

There is another reason we don't communicate face-to-face. We don't want to have the other guy see the inner machinations of our team. Think about what the scribe does, for example. If by some chance the bad guy would even surmise that someone is writing down information about him, he might not just feel threatened. After all, if you have someone who's barricaded or holding hostages, he's going to be highly paranoid about his safety.

What's the most dangerous negotiation situation?

Generally speaking, suicide is the most dangerous situation because it's the most volatile. There's no suffering for people who are threatening suicide. By the time they get this far, they have finished suffering. So unlike criminals who are facing a jail term, suicidal people fear nothing. They're not worried that they might be punished for what they're doing to themselves—or to you. They're just not thinking. And, as we've seen with the suicide bombers in Israel, that makes them some of the most dangerous people we could ever deal with.

Once I had a suicidal ex—police officer who had climbed to the top of the Whitestone Bridge. A lot of people who saw her said, "Aw, she's up there just because she wants the publicity." But I never believed that. It was clear to me that she had emotional problems. Her therapist came to the scene after I had talked her down, and he told the team that we had handled her perfectly because we understood intuitively how dangerous she was. In fact, he told us, she was not only suicidal; she was homicidal. "She wouldn't have hesitated, if you made her mad, to grab one of you and take you over the bridge with her." Incidentally, suicide is the main reason we never allow a priest or a rabbi to talk to a bad guy. We have learned over and over that when people ask for clergy, they are virtually always looking for closure on their lives. It's a prelude to suicide.

What's the biggest lesson you have learned from your work as a crisis negotiator?

I don't know if it's the biggest lesson, but one very important thing you learn as a negotiator is that if you want to win, you have to help the other guy to save face. Look at the people I deal with. They're criminals. They're not book-learned. Yet they're very smart in the sense that they can survive in an environment where most of us cannot, and they also have their own kind of dignity. If you can show these guys a way to maintain their pride while facing a defeat they know is inevitable, they'll go along with what you want.

I learned that lesson early in my negotiation career when I was called in to deal with a situation in Spanish Harlem. It was a hot summer night, and there were 300 or 400 people out on the streets at three o'clock in the morning. A young man with a loaded shotgun had blockaded himself inside a crowded tenement building. He told me he wanted to surrender but couldn't because he'd look weak.

Now this guy was a parole violator, not a murderer, and so I told him that if he calmed down and let me cuff him, I would make it look as if I had to use force. He put down his gun and behaved like a perfect gentleman until we got to the street, where he started screaming like crazy and raising hell, as we had agreed. While he was doing this, the crowd was chanting "Jose!" in wild approval, and we threw him into the back of the car, jumped on the gas, and sped off. Two blocks later, José sat up, broke into a huge grin, and said to me, "Hey man, thank you. I really appreciated that." He recognized that I had given him a way out that didn't involve killing people and being killed in turn. I've never forgotten that.

DOMINICK MISINO is a former NYPD detective and hostage negotiator, acclaimed in 1993 for persuading the hijacker of Lufthansa Flight 592 to surrender peacefully. DIANE L. COUTU is a former senior editor of *Harvard Business Review*.

Originally published in October 2002. Reprint R0210C

Six Habits of Merely Effective Negotiators

by James K. Sebenius

GLOBAL DEAL MAKERS DID a staggering $3.3 trillion worth of M&A transactions in 1999—and that's only a fraction of the capital that passed through negotiators' hands that year. Behind the deal-driven headlines, executives endlessly negotiate with customers and suppliers, with large shareholders and creditors, with prospective joint venture and alliance partners, with people inside their companies and across national borders. Indeed, wherever parties with different interests and perceptions depend on each other for results, negotiation matters. Little wonder that Bob Davis, vice chairman of Terra Lycos, has said that companies "have to make deal making a core competency."

Luckily, whether from schoolbooks or the school of hard knocks, most executives know the basics of negotiation; some are spectacularly adept. Yet high stakes and intense pressure can result in costly mistakes. Bad habits creep in, and experience can further ingrain those habits. Indeed, when I reflect on the thousands of negotiations I have participated in and studied over the years, I'm struck by how frequently even experienced negotiators leave money on the table, deadlock, damage relationships, or allow conflict to spiral. (For more on the rich theoretical understanding of negotiations developed by researchers over the past fifty years, see the sidebar "Academics Take a Seat at the Negotiating Table.")

There are as many specific reasons for bad outcomes in negotiations as there are individuals and deals. Yet broad classes of errors recur. In this article, I'll explore those mistakes, comparing good negotiating practice with bad. But first, let's take a closer look at the right negotiation problem that your approach must solve.

Solving the Right Negotiation Problem

In any negotiation, each side ultimately must choose between two options: accepting a deal or taking its best no-deal option—that is, the course of action it would take if the deal were not possible. As a negotiator, you seek to advance the full set of your interests by persuading the other side to say yes—and mean it—to a proposal that meets your interests better than your best no-deal option does. And why should the other side say yes? Because the deal meets its own interests better than its best no-deal option. So, while protecting your own choice, your negotiation problem is to understand and shape your counterpart's perceived decision—deal versus no deal—so that

Idea in Brief

High stakes. Intense pressure. Careless mistakes. These can turn your key negotiations into disasters. Even seasoned negotiators bungle deals, leaving money on the table and damaging working relationships.

Why? During negotiations, six common mistakes can distract you from your *real* purpose: getting the other guy to choose what you want—for *his* own reasons.

Avoid negotiation pitfalls by mastering the art of letting the other guy have your way— *everyone* will win.

the other side chooses *in its own interest* what you want. As Italian diplomat Daniele Vare said long ago about diplomacy, negotiation is "the art of letting them have your way."

This approach may seem on the surface like a recipe for manipulation. But in fact, understanding your counterpart's interests and shaping the decision so the other side agrees for its own reasons is the key to jointly creating and claiming sustainable value from a negotiation. Yet even experienced negotiators make six common mistakes that keep them from solving the right problem.

Mistake 1: Neglecting the Other Side's Problem

You can't negotiate effectively unless you understand your own interests and your own no-deal options. So far, so good—but there's much more to it than that. Since the other side will say yes for its reasons, not yours, agreement requires understanding and addressing your counterpart's problem as a means to solving your own.

Idea in Pracitce

Negotiation Mistakes

Neglecting the other side's problem

If you don't understand the deal from the other side's perspective, you can't solve his problem *or* yours.

> *Example:* A technology company that created a cheap, accurate way of detecting gas-tank leaks couldn't sell its product. Why? EPA regulations permitted leaks of up to 1,500 gallons, while this new technology detected *8-ounce* leaks. Fearing the device would spawn regulatory trouble, potential customers said, "No deal!"

Letting price bulldoze other interests

Most deals involve interests *besides* price:

- a positive working relationship, crucial in longer-term deals
- the social contract, or "spirit of the deal,"

including goodwill and shared expectations

- the deal-making process—personal, respectful, and fair to both sides

Price-centric tactics leave these potential *joint* gains unrealized.

Letting positions drive out interests

Incompatible *positions* may mask compatible *interests*. Your gain isn't necessarily your "opponent's" loss.

> *Example:* Environmentalists and farmers opposed a power company's proposed dam. Yet compatible *interests* underlay these seemingly irreconcilable positions: Farmers wanted water flow; environmentalists, wildlife protection; the power company, a greener image. By agreeing to a smaller dam, water-flow guarantees, and habitat conservation, everyone won.

At a minimum, you need to understand the problem from the other side's perspective. Consider a technology company, whose board of directors pressed hard to develop a hot new product shortly after it went

Searching too hard for common ground

While common ground helps negotiations, *different* interests can give each party what it values most, at minimum cost to the other.

> *Example:* An acquirer and entrepreneur disagree on the entrepreneurial company's likely future. To satisfy their differing interests, the buyer agrees to pay a fixed amount now and contingent amount later, based on future performance. Both find the deal more attractive than walking away.

Neglecting BATNA

BATNAs ("best alternative to a negotiated agreement") represent your actions if the proposed deal weren't possible; e.g., walk away, approach another buyer. Assessing your own *and* your partner's BATNA reveals surprising possibilities.

> *Example:* A company hoping to sell a struggling division for somewhat more than its $7 million value had two fiercely competitive bidders. Speculating each might pay an inflated price to trump the other, the seller ensured each knew its rival was looking. The division's selling price? *$45 million.*

Failing to correct for skewed vision

Two forms of bias can prompt errors:

- *Role bias*—overcommitting to your own point of view and interpreting information in self-serving ways. A plaintiff believes he has a 70% chance of winning his case, while the defense puts the odds at 50%. Result? Unlikelihood of out-of-court settlement.

- *Partisan perceptions*—painting your side with positive qualities, while vilifying your "opponent." Self-fulfilling prophecies may result.

Counteract these biases with role-plays of the opposition's interests.

public. The company had developed a technology for detecting leaks in underground gas tanks that was both cheaper and about 100 times more accurate than existing technologies—at a time when the Environmental

Academics Take a Seat at the Negotiating Table

PARALLELING THE GROWTH IN real-world negotiation, several generations of researchers have deepened our understanding of the process. In the 1950s and 1960s, elements of hard (win-lose) bargaining were isolated and refined: how to set aggressive targets, start high, concede slowly, and employ threats, bluffs, and commitments to positions without triggering an impasse or escalation. By the early 1980s, with the win-win revolution popularized by the book *Getting to Yes* (by Roger Fisher, William Ury, and Bruce Patton), the focus shifted from battling over the division of the pie to the means of expanding it by uncovering and reconciling underlying interests. More sophisticated analysis in Howard Raiffa's *Art and Science of Negotiation* soon transcended this simplistic "win-win versus win-lose" debate; the pie obviously had to be both expanded and divided. In *The Manager as Negotiator* (by David Lax and James Sebenius), new guidance emerged on productively managing the tension between the cooperative moves necessary to create value and the competitive moves involved in claiming it. As the 1990s progressed with work such as *Negotiating Rationally* (by Max Bazerman and Margaret Neale), the behavioral study of negotiation—describing how people actually negotiate—began to merge with the game theoretic approach, which prescribed how fully rational people should negotiate. This new synthesis—developing the best possible advice without assuming strictly rational behavior—is producing rich insights in negotiations ranging from simple two-party, one-shot, single-issue situations through complex coalitional dealings over multiple issues over time, where internal negotiations must be synchronized with external ones. Negotiation courses that explore these ideas have always been popular options at business schools, but reflecting the growing recognition of their importance, these courses are beginning to be required as part of MBA core programs at schools such as Harvard. Rather than a special skill for making major deals or resolving disputes, negotiation has become a way of life for effective executives.

Protection Agency was persuading Congress to mandate that these tanks be continuously tested. Not surprisingly, the directors thought their timing was perfect and pushed employees to commercialize and market the technology in time to meet the demand. To their dismay, the company's first sale turned out to be its only one. Quite a mystery, since the technology worked, the product was less expensive, and the regulations did come through. Imagine the sales engineers confidently negotiating with a customer for a new order: "This technology costs less and is more accurate than the competition's." Think for a moment, though, about how intended buyers might mull over their interests, especially given that EPA regulations permitted leaks of up to 1,500 gallons while the new technology could pick up an 0 ounce leak. Potential buyer: "What a technological tour de force! This handy new device will almost certainly get me into needless, expensive regulatory trouble. And create P.R. problems too. I think I'll pass, but my competition should definitely have it." From the technology company's perspective, "faster, better, cheaper" added up to a sure deal; to the other side, it looked like a headache. No deal.

Social psychologists have documented the difficulty most people have understanding the other side's perspective. From the trenches, successful negotiators concur that overcoming this self-centered tendency is critical. As Millennium Pharmaceuticals' Steve Holtzman put it after a string of deals vaulted his company from a start-up in 1993 to a major player with a $10.6 billion market cap today, "We spend a lot of time thinking about how the poor guy or woman on the other side of the table is going to have to go sell this deal to his or her boss. We spend a lot of time trying to understand how they are modeling it." And Wayne Huizenga, veteran of more than a thousand deals building Waste Management, AutoNation, and Blockbuster, distilled his extensive experience into basic advice that is often heard but even more often forgotten. "In all my years of doing deals, a few rules and lessons have emerged. Most important, always try to put yourself in the other person's shoes. It's vital to try to understand in depth what the other side really wants out of the deal."

Tough negotiators sometimes see the other side's concerns but dismiss them: "That's their problem and their issue. Let them handle it. We'll look after our own problems." This attitude can undercut your ability to profitably influence how your counterpart sees its problem. Early in his deal-making career at Cisco Systems, Mike Volpi, now chief strategy officer, had trouble completing proposed deals, his "outward confidence" often mistaken for arrogance. Many acquisitions later, a colleague observed that "the most important part of [Volpi's] development is that he learned power doesn't come from telling people you are powerful. He went from being a guy driving the deal from his side of the table to the guy who understood the deal from the other side."

An associate of Rupert Murdoch remarked that, as a buyer, Murdoch "understands the seller—and, whatever the guy's trying to do, he crafts his offer that way." If you want to change someone's mind, you should first learn where that person's mind is. Then, together, you can try to build what my colleague Bill Ury calls a "golden bridge," spanning the gulf between where your counterpart is now and your desired end point. This is much more effective than trying to shove the other side from its position to yours. As an eighteenth-century pope once noted about Cardinal de Polignac's remarkable diplomatic skills, "This young man always seems to be of my opinion [at the start of a negotiation], and at the end of the conversation I find that I am of his." In short, the first mistake is to focus on your own problem, exclusively. Solve the other side's as the means to solving your own.

Mistake 2; Letting Price Bulldoze Other Interests

Negotiators who pay attention exclusively to price turn potentially cooperative deals into adversarial ones. These "reverse Midas" negotiators, as I like to call them, use hard-bargaining tactics that often leave potential joint gains unrealized. That's because, while price is an important factor in most deals, it's rarely the only one. As Felix Rohatyn, former managing partner of the investment bank, Lazard Frères, observed, "Most deals are 50% emotion and 50% economics."

There's a large body of research to support Rohatyn's view. Consider, for example, a simplified negotiation, extensively studied in academic labs, involving real money. One party is given, say, $100 to divide with another party as she likes; the second party can agree or disagree to the arrangement. If he agrees, the $100 is divided in line with the first side's proposal; if not, neither party gets anything. A pure price logic would suggest proposing something like $99 for me, $1 for you. Although this is an extreme allocation, it still represents a position in which your counterpart gets something rather than nothing. Pure price negotiators confidently predict the other side will agree to the split; after all, they've been offered free money—it's like finding a dollar on the street and putting it in your pocket. Who wouldn't pick it up?

In reality, however, most players turn down proposals that don't let them share in at least 35% to 40% of the bounty—even when much larger stakes are involved and the amount they forfeit is significant. While these rejections are "irrational" on a pure price basis and virtually incomprehensible to reverse Midas types, studies show that when a split feels too unequal to people, they reject the spoils as unfair, are offended by the process, and perhaps try to teach the "greedy" person a lesson.

An important real-world message is embedded in these lab results: people care about much more than the absolute level of their own economic outcome; competing interests include relative results, perceived fairness, self-image, reputation, and so on. Successful negotiators, acknowledging that economics aren't everything, focus on four important nonprice factors.

The Relationship
Less experienced negotiators often undervalue the importance of developing working relationships with the other parties, putting the relationships at risk by overly

tough tactics or simple neglect. This is especially true in cross-border deals. In much of Latin America, southern Europe, and Southeast Asia, for example, relationships—rather than transactions—can be the predominant negotiating interest when working out longer term deals. Results-oriented North Americans, Northern Europeans, and Australians often come to grief by underestimating the strength of this interest and insisting prematurely that the negotiators "get down to business."

The Social Contract

Similarly, negotiators tend to focus on the economic contract—equity splits, cost sharing, governance, and so on—at the expense of the social contract or the "spirit of a deal." Going well beyond a good working relationship, the social contract governs people's expectations about the nature, extent, and duration of the venture, about process, and about the way unforeseen events will be handled. Especially in new ventures and strategic alliances, where goodwill and strong shared expectations are extremely important, negotiating a positive social contract is an important way to reinforce economic contracts. Scurrying to check founding documents when conflicts occur, which they inevitably do, can signal a badly negotiated social contract.

The Process

Negotiators often forget that the deal-making process can be as important as its content. The story is told of the young Tip O'Neill, who later became Speaker of the House, meeting an elderly constituent on the streets of his North Cambridge, Massachusetts, district. Surprised to learn that she was not planning to vote for him, O'Neill probed, "Haven't you known me and my family all my life?" "Yes." "Haven't I cut your grass in summer and shoveled your walk in winter?" "Yes." "Don't you agree with all my policies and positions?" "Yes." "Then why aren't you going to vote for me?" "Because you didn't ask me to." Considerable academic research confirms what O'Neill learned from this conversation: process counts. What's more, sustainable results are more often reached when all parties perceive the process as personal, respectful, straightforward, and fair.[1]

The Interests of the Full Set of Players

Less experienced negotiators sometimes become mesmerized by the aggregate economics of a deal and forget about the interests of players who are in a position to torpedo it. When the boards of pharmaceutical giants Glaxo and SmithKline Beecham publicly announced their merger in 1998, investors were thrilled, rapidly *increasing* the combined company's market capitalization by a stunning $20 billion. Yet despite prior agreement on who would occupy which top executive positions in the newly combined company, internal disagreement about management control and position resurfaced and sank the announced deal, and the $20 billion evaporated. (Overwhelming strategic logic ultimately drove the companies back together, but only after nearly two years had passed.) This episode confirms two related lessons. First, while favorable overall economics are generally necessary, they are often not sufficient. Second, keep all potentially influential internal players on your radar screen; don't lose sight of their interests or their capacity to affect the deal. What is "rational" for the whole may not be so for the parts.

It can be devilishly difficult to cure the reverse Midas touch. If you treat a potentially cooperative negotiation like a pure price deal, it will likely become one. Imagine a negotiator who expects a hardball, price-driven process. She initiates the bid by taking a tough preemptive position; the other side is likely to reciprocate. "Aha!" says the negotiator, her suspicions confirmed. "I *knew* this was just going to be a tough price deal."

A negotiator can often influence whether price will dominate or be kept in perspective. Consider negotiations between two companies trying to establish an equity joint venture. Among other issues, they are trying to place a value on each side's contribution to determine ownership shares. A negotiator might drive this process down two very different paths. A price-focused approach quickly isolates the valuation issue and then bangs out a resolution. Alternatively, the two sides could first flesh out a more specific shared vision for the joint venture (together envisioning the "pot of gold" they could create), probe to understand the most critical concerns of each side—including price—and craft trade-offs among the full set of issues to meet these interests. In the latter approach, price becomes a component or even an implication of a larger, longer term package, rather than the primary focus.

Some negotiations are indeed pure price deals and only about aggregate economics, but there is often much more to work with. Wise negotiators put the vital issue of price in perspective and don't straitjacket their view of the richer interests at stake. They work with the subjective as well as the objective, with the process and the relationship, with the "social contract" or spirit of a deal as well as its letter, and with the interests of the parts as well as the whole.

Mistake 3: Letting Positions Drive Out Interests

Three elements are at play in a negotiation. *Issues* are on the table for explicit agreement. *Positions* are one party's stands on the issues. *Interests* are underlying concerns that would be affected by the resolution. Of course, positions on issues reflect underlying interests, but they need not be identical. Suppose you're considering a job offer. The base salary will probably be an issue. Perhaps your position on that issue is that you need to earn $100,000. The interests underlying that position include your need for a good income but may also include status, security, new opportunities, and needs that can be met in ways other than salary. Yet even very experienced deal makers may see the essence of negotiation as a dance of positions. If incompatible positions finally converge, a deal is struck; if not, the negotiation ends in an impasse. By contrast, interest-driven bargainers see the process primarily as a reconciliation of underlying interests: you have one set of interests, I have another, and through joint problem solving we should be better able to meet both sets of interests and thus create new value.

Consider a dispute over a dam project. Environmentalists and farmers opposed a U.S. power company's plans to build a dam. The two sides had irreconcilable positions: "absolutely yes" and "no way." Yet these incompatible positions masked compatible interests. The farmers were worried about reduced water flow below the dam, the environmentalists were focused on the downstream habitat of the endangered whooping crane, and the power company needed new capacity and a greener image. After a costly legal stalemate, the three groups devised an interest-driven agreement that all of them considered preferable to continued court warfare. The agreement included a smaller dam built on a fast track, water flow guarantees, downstream habitat protection, and a trust fund to enhance whooping crane habitats elsewhere.

Despite the clear advantages of reconciling deeper interests, people have a built-in bias toward focusing on their own positions instead. This hardwired assumption that our interests are incompatible implies a zero-sum pie in which my gain is your loss. Research in psychology supports the mythical fixed-pie view as the norm. In a survey of 5,000 subjects in 32 negotiating studies, mostly carried out with monetary stakes, participants failed to realize compatible issues fully half of the time.[2] In real-world terms, this means that enormous value is unknowingly left uncreated as both sides walk away from money on the table.

Reverse Midas negotiators, for example, almost automatically fixate on price and bargaining positions to claim value. After the usual preliminaries, countless negotiations get serious when one side asks, "so, what's your position," or says, "here's my position." This positional approach often drives the process toward a ritual value-claiming dance. Great negotiators understand that the dance of bargaining positions is only the surface game; the real action takes place when they've probed behind positions for the full set of interests at stake. Reconciling interests to create value requires patience and a willingness to research the other side, ask many questions, and listen. It would be silly to write off either price or bargaining position; both are extremely important. And there is, of course, a limit to joint value creation. The trick is to recognize and productively manage the tension between cooperative actions needed to create value and competitive ones needed to claim it. The pie must be both expanded and divided.

Mistake 4: Searching Too Hard for Common Ground

Conventional wisdom says we negotiate to overcome the differences that divide us. So, typically, we're advised to find win-win agreements by searching for common ground. Common ground is generally a good thing. Yet many of the most frequently overlooked sources of value in negotiation arise from differences among the parties.

Recall the battle over the dam. The solution—a smaller dam, water flow guarantees, habitat conservation—did not result from common interests but because farmers, environmentalists, and the utility had different priorities. Similarly, when Egypt and Israel were negotiating over the Sinai, their positions on where to draw the boundary were incompatible. When negotiators went beyond the opposing positions, however, they uncovered a vital difference of underlying interest and priority: the Israelis cared more about security, while the Egyptians cared more about sovereignty. The solution was a demilitarized zone under the Egyptian flag. Differences of interest or priority can open the door to unbundling different elements and giving each party what it values the most—at the least cost to the other.

Even when an issue seems purely economic, finding differences can break open deadlocked deals. Consider a small technology company and its investors, stuck in a tough negotiation with a large strategic acquirer adamant about paying much less than the asking price. On investigation, it turned out that the acquirer was actually willing to pay the higher price but was concerned about raising price expectations in a fast-moving sector in which it planned to make more acquisitions. The solution was for the two sides to agree on a modest, well-publicized initial cash purchase price; the deal included complex-sounding contingencies that virtually guaranteed a much higher price later.

Differences in forecasts can also fuel joint gains. Suppose an entrepreneur who is genuinely optimistic about the prospects of her fast-growing company faces a potential buyer who likes the company but is much more skeptical about the company's future cash flow. They have

Solving Teddy Roosevelt's Negotiation Problem

THEODORE ROOSEVELT, NEARING THE end of a hard-fought presidential election campaign in 1912, scheduled a final whistle-stop journey. At each stop, Roosevelt planned to clinch the crowd's votes by distributing an elegant pamphlet with a stern presidential portrait on the cover and a stirring speech, "Confession of Faith," inside. Some three million copies had been printed when a campaign worker noticed a small line under the photograph on each brochure that read, "Moffett Studios, Chicago." Since Moffett held the copyright, the unauthorized use of the photo could cost the campaign one dollar per reproduction. With no time to reprint the brochure, what was the campaign to do?

Not using the pamphlets at all would damage Roosevelt's election prospects. Yet, if they went ahead, a scandal could easily erupt very close to the election, and the campaign could be liable for an unaffordable sum. Campaign workers quickly realized they would have to negotiate with Moffett. But research by their Chicago operatives turned up bad news: although early in his career as a photographer, Moffett had been taken with the potential of this new artistic medium, he had received little recognition. Now, Moffett was financially hard up and bitterly approaching retirement with a single-minded focus on money.

Dispirited, the campaign workers approached campaign manager George Perkins, a former partner of J.P. Morgan. Perkins lost no time summoning his stenographer to dispatch the following cable to Moffett Studios: "We are planning to distribute millions of pamphlets with Roosevelt's picture on the cover. It will be great publicity for the studio whose photograph we use. How much will you pay us to use yours? Respond immediately." Shortly, Moffett replied: "We've never done this before, but under the circumstances we'd be pleased to offer you $250." Reportedly, Perkins accepted—without dickering for more.

Perkins's misleading approach raises ethical yellow flags and is anything but a model negotiation on how to enhance working relationships. Yet this case raises a very interesting question: why did the campaign workers find the prospect of this negotiation so difficult? Their inability to see what Perkins immediately perceived flowed from their anxious obsession with their own side's problem: their blunders so far, the high risk of losing the election, a potential $3 million exposure, an urgent deadline, and no cash to meet Moffett's likely demands for something the campaign vitally needed. Had they avoided mistake 1 by pausing for a moment and thinking about how Moffett saw his problem, they would have realized that Moffett didn't even know he had a problem. Perkins's tactical genius was to recognize the essence of the negotiator's central task: shape how your counterpart sees its problem such that it chooses what you want.

The campaign workers were paralyzed in the face of what they saw as sharply conflicting monetary interests and their pathetic BATNA. From their perspective, Moffett's only choice was how to exploit their desperation at the prospect of losing the presidency. By contrast, dodging mistake 5, Perkins immediately grasped the importance of favorably shaping Moffett's BATNA perceptions, both of the campaign's (awful) no-deal options and Moffett's (powerful) one. Perkins looked beyond price, positions, and common ground (mistakes 2, 3, and 4) and used Moffett's different interests to frame the photographer's choice as "the value of publicity and recognition." Had he assumed this would be a standard, hardball price deal by offering a small amount to start, not only would this assumption have been dead wrong but, worse, it would have been self-fulfilling.

Risky and ethically problematic? Yes ... but Perkins saw his options as certain disaster versus some chance of avoiding it. And was Moffett really entitled to a $3 million windfall, avoidable had the campaign caught its oversight a week beforehand? Hard to say, but this historical footnote, which I've greatly embellished, illuminates the intersection of negotiating mistakes, tactics, and ethics.

negotiated in good faith, but, at the end of the day, the two sides sharply disagree on the likely future of the company and so cannot find an acceptable sale price. Instead of seeing these different forecasts as a barrier, a savvy negotiator could use them to bridge the value gap by proposing a deal in which the buyer pays a fixed amount now and a contingent amount later on the basis of the company's future performance. Properly structured with adequate incentives and monitoring mechanisms, such a contingent payment, or "earn-out," can appear quite valuable to the optimistic seller—who expects to get her higher valuation—but not very costly to the less optimistic buyer. And willingness to accept such a contingent deal may signal that the seller's confidence in the business is genuine. Both may find the deal much more attractive than walking away.

A host of other differences make up the raw material for joint gains. A less risk-averse party can "insure" a more risk-averse one. An impatient party can get most of the early money, while his more patient counterpart can get considerably more over a longer period of time. Differences in cost or revenue structure, tax status, or regulatory arrangements between two parties can be converted into gains for both. Indeed, conducting a disciplined "differences inventory" is at least as important a task as is identifying areas of common ground. After all, if we were all clones of one another, with the same interests, beliefs, attitudes toward risk and time, assets, and so on, there would be little to negotiate. While common ground helps, differences drive deals. But negotiators who don't actively search for differences rarely find them.

Mistake 5: Neglecting BATNAs

BATNAs—the acronym for "best alternative to a negotiated agreement" coined years ago by Roger Fisher, Bill
Ury, and Bruce Patton in their book *Getting to Yes*—reflect
the course of action a party would take if the proposed
deal were not possible. A BATNA may involve walking
away, prolonging a stalemate, approaching another potential buyer, making something in-house rather than
procuring it externally, going to court rather than set-
tling, forming a different alliance, or going on strike.
BATNAs set the threshold—in terms of the full set of interests—that any acceptable agreement must exceed.
Both parties doing better than their BATNAs is a necessary condition for an agreement. Thus BATNAs define a
zone of possible agreement and determine its location.

A strong BATNA is an important negotiation tool.
Many people associate the ability to inflict or withstand
damage with bargaining power, but your willingness to
walk away to an apparently good BATNA is often more
important. The better your BATNA appears both to you
and to the other party, the more credible your threat to
walk away becomes, and the more it can serve as leverage to improve the deal. Roger Fisher has dramatized
this point by asking which you would prefer to have in
your back pocket during a compensation negotiation
with your boss: a gun or a terrific job offer from a desirable employer who is also a serious competitor of your
company?

Not only should you assess your own BATNA, you
should also think carefully about the other side's. Doing

so can alert you to surprising possibilities. In one instance, a British company hoped to sell a poorly performing division for a bit more than its depreciated asset value of $7 million to one of two potential buyers. Realizing that these buyers were fierce rivals in other markets, the seller speculated that each party might be willing to pay an inflated price to keep the other from getting the division. So they made sure that each suitor knew the other was looking and skillfully cultivated the interest of both companies. The division sold for $45 million.

Negotiators must also be careful not to inadvertently damage their BATNAs. I saw that happen at a Canadian chemical manufacturing company that had decided to sell a large but nonstrategic division to raise urgently needed cash. The CEO charged his second-in-command with negotiating the sale of the division at the highest possible price.

The target buyer was an Australian company, whose chief executive was an old school friend of the Canadian CEO. The Australian chief executive let it be known that his company was interested in the deal but that his senior management was consumed, at the moment, with other priorities. If the Australian company could have a nine-month negotiating exclusive to "confirm their seriousness about the sale," the Australian chief executive would dedicate the top personnel to make the deal happen. A chief-to-chief agreement to that effect was struck. Pity the second-in-command, charged with urgently maximizing cash from this sale, as he jetted off to Sydney with no meaningful alternative for nine endless months to whatever price the Australians offered.

Negotiators often become preoccupied with tactics, trying to improve the potential deal while neglecting their own BATNA and that of the other side. Yet the real negotiation problem is "deal versus BATNA," not one or the other in isolation. Your potential deal and your BATNA should work together as the two blades of the scissors do to cut a piece of paper.

Mistake 6: Failing to Correct for Skewed Vision

You may be crystal clear on the right negotiation problem—but you can't solve it correctly without a firm understanding of both sides' interests, BATNAs, valuations, likely actions, and so on. Yet, just as a pilot's sense of the horizon at night or in a storm can be wildly inaccurate, the psychology of perception systematically leads negotiators to major errors.[3]

Self-Serving Role Bias

People tend unconsciously to interpret information pertaining to their own side in a strongly self-serving way. The following experiment shows the process at work. Harvard researchers gave a large group of executives financial and industry information about one company negotiating to acquire another. The executive subjects were randomly assigned to the negotiating roles of buyer or seller; the information provided to each side was identical. After plenty of time for analysis, all subjects were asked for their private assessment of the target company's fair value—as distinct from how they might portray that value in the bargaining process.

Those assigned the role of seller gave median valuations more than twice those given by the executives assigned to the buyer's role. These valuation gulfs had no basis in fact; they were driven entirely by random role assignments.

Even comparatively modest role biases can blow up potential deals. Suppose a plaintiff believes he has a 70% chance of winning a million-dollar judgment, while the defense thinks the plaintiff has only a 50% chance of winning. This means that, in settlement talks, the plaintiff's expected BATNA for a court battle (to get $700,000 minus legal fees) will exceed the defendant's assessment of his exposure (to pay $500,000 plus fees). Without significant risk aversion, the divergent assessments would block any out-of-court settlement. This cognitive role bias helps explain why Microsoft took such a confrontational approach in its recent struggle with the U.S. Department of Justice. The company certainly appeared overoptimistic about its chances in court. Similarly, Arthur Andersen likely exhibited overconfidence in its arbitration prospects over the terms of separation from Andersen Consulting (now Accenture). Getting too committed to your point of view—"believing your own line"—is an extremely common mistake.

Partisan Perceptions

While we systematically err in processing information critical to our own side, we are even worse at assessing the other side—especially in an adversarial situation. Extensive research has documented an unconscious mechanism that enhances one's own side, "portraying it as more talented, honest, and morally upright," while simultaneously vilifying the opposition. This often leads to exaggerated perceptions of the other side's position and overestimates of the actual substantive conflict. To an outsider, those caught up in disintegrating partnerships or marriages often appear to hold exaggerated views of each other. Such partisan perceptions can become even more virulent among people on each side of divides, such as Israelis and Palestinians, Bosnian Muslims and the Serbs, or Catholics and Protestants in Northern Ireland.

Partisan perceptions can easily become self-fulfilling prophecies. Experiments testing the effects of teachers' expectations of students, psychiatrists' diagnoses of mental patients, and platoon leaders' expectations of their trainees confirm the notion that partisan perceptions often shape behavior. At the negotiating table, clinging firmly to the idea that one's counterpart is stubborn or extreme, for example, is likely to trigger just that behavior, sharply reducing the possibility of reaching a constructive agreement.

As disagreement and conflict intensify, sophisticated negotiators should expect biased perceptions, both on their own side and the other side. Less seasoned players tend to be shocked and outraged by perceived extremism and are wholly unaware that their own views are likely colored by their roles. How to counteract these powerful biases? Just knowing that they exist helps. Seeking the views of outside, uninvolved parties is useful, too. And having people on your side prepare the strongest possible case for the other side can serve as the basis for preparatory role-playing that can generate valuable insights. A few years ago, helping a client get ready for a tough deal, I suggested that the client create a detailed "brief" for each side and have the team's best people negotiate for the other side in a reverse role-play. The brief for my client's side was lengthy, eloquent, and persuasive. Tellingly, the brief describing the other side's situation was only two pages long and consisted mainly of reasons for conceding quickly to my client's superior arguments. Not only were my client's executives fixated on their own problem (mistake 1), their perceptions of each side were also hopelessly biased (mistake 6). To prepare effectively, they needed to undertake significant competitive research and reality-test their views with uninvolved outsiders.

From Merely Effective to Superior Negotiation

So you have navigated the shoals of merely effective deal making to face what is truly the right problem. You have focused on the full set of interests of all parties, rather than fixating on price and positions. You have looked beyond common ground to unearth value-creating differences. You have assessed and shaped BATNAs. You have taken steps to avoid role biases and partisan perceptions. In short, you have grasped your own problem clearly and have sought to understand and influence the other side's such that what it chooses is what you want.

Plenty of errors still lie in wait: cultural gaffes, an irritating style, inadvertent signals of disrespect or untrustworthiness, miscommunication, bad timing, revealing too much or too little, a poorly designed agenda, sequencing mistakes, negotiating with the wrong person on the other side, personalizing issues, and so on. Even if you manage to avoid these mistakes as well, you may still run into difficulties by approaching the negotiation far too narrowly, taking too many of the elements of the "problem" as fixed.

The very best negotiators take a broader approach to setting up and solving the right problem. With a keen sense of the potential value to be created as their guiding beacon, these negotiators are game-changing entrepreneurs. They envision the most promising architecture and take action to bring it into being. These virtuoso negotiators not only play the game as given at the table, they are masters at setting it up and changing it away from the table to maximize the chances for better results.

To advance the full set of their interests, they understand and shape the other side's choice—deal versus no deal—such that the other chooses what they want. As François de Callières, an eighteenth-century commentator, once put it, negotiation masters possess "the supreme art of making every man offer him as a gift that which it was his chief design to secure."

Notes

1. W. Chan Kim and Renée Mauborgne, "Fair Process: Managing in the Knowledge Economy," HBR July–August 1997.

2. This and other studies illustrating this point can be found in Leigh Thompson's *The Mind and Heart of the Negotiator* (Prentice Hall, 1998).

3. See Robert J. Robinson, "Errors in Social Judgment: Implications for Negotiation and Conflict Resolution, Part I: Biased Assimilation of

Information," Harvard Business School, 1997 and Robert J. Robinson, "Errors in Social Judgment: Implications for Negotiation and Conflict Resolution, Part II: Partisan Perceptions," Harvard Business School, 1997.

JAMES K. SEBENIUS is the Gordon Donaldson Professor of Business Administration at Harvard Business School, where he led the creation of the negotiation unit.

Originally published in April 2001. Reprint R0104E

The Fine Art of Friendly Acquisition

by Robert J. Aiello and Michael D. Watkins

A RECENT STUDY ON M&A turned up a surprising statistic. Between 1984 and 1994, some 80% of LBO firms reported that their fund investors had received a return that matched or exceeded their cost of capital, even though in many cases the prices paid for the companies those funds acquired were pushed up by competing bidders. That figure stands in stark contrast to the overall record of M&A investments, which from the corporate acquirer's perspective has been dismal, at times disastrous.

The fact that financial acquirers are so much more successful than most corporate acquirers may come as a shock to some managers. After all, financial investors don't bring synergies to their acquisitions, and they often have relatively little operational experience in the industries involved. Indeed, it's highly likely that the target's management team will initially view potential acquirers with substantial skepticism.[1]

Why, then, are financial acquirers so successful? Based on our experience advising companies on both acquisitions and negotiation strategy, we believe the answer lies in their approach to the acquisition process. Most corporate managers treat acquisitions as a direct-march-up-the-hill kind of exercise: "I want to buy this company. Let's find out what it's worth, offer less, and see if we get it." The actual deal-management process is often delegated to outside experts—to investment bankers and lawyers.

But senior managers at financial investors—and the more successful corporate acquirers—treat deal management as a core part of their business. They approach potential acquisitions with sensitivity and a well-established process. They adjust their negotiating postures and objectives as the deal evolves. And they take the trouble to carefully coordinate the different actors—senior managers, lawyers, investment bankers, and so on—throughout the process. It is this care and effort that enables successful acquirers to create the value they do.

In this article, we'll describe how successful acquirers manage their deals. Our focus is primarily on friendly deals, but much of what we found is applicable in a hostile context as well because even a hostile bid has to end in an agreement to work together. All friendly M&A deals pass through five distinct stages: screening potential deals, reaching an initial agreement, conducting due diligence, setting the final agreement, and ultimately closing. We'll walk you through that process, comparing good practice with bad, and

Idea in Brief

It's no secret that the track record of corporate acquirers has been dismal. But there is a group that's had consistent success. A recent study on M&A reveals that between 1984 and 1994, fund investors at some 80% of LBO firms enjoyed returns equal to or greater than their cost of capital on their M&A investments. And this was true even though in many cases the prices paid for the companies were pushed up by competing bidders. Why are financial acquirers so much more successful than their corporate counterparts? It's because they approach the negotiation process differently. Fund investors treat deal management as a core part of their business conducted by a permanent group of experienced executives, and they have well-established processes that they stick to. The authors examine how the best acquirers approach all five stages of deal negotiations—screening potential deals, reaching initial agreement, conducting due diligence, setting final terms, and reaching closure—comparing good practice with bad, to reveal the secrets of their success.

then we'll suggest ways companies can turn their deal-making experiences into organizational learning.

Screening Potential Deals

Acquisition possibilities can pop up without warning and usually need to be evaluated quickly. A core challenge in sizing up potential acquisitions, therefore, is to balance the need to think strategically with the need to react opportunistically. Experienced acquirers follow two simple rules in screening deals.

Look at Everything

Successful acquirers are always on the lookout for deals. An LBO shop such as the New York City-based Cypress

Group might complete only two or three deals a year, but it will have explored as many as 500 possibilities and have closely examined perhaps 25 of them. Successful corporate acquirers do much the same, albeit on a smaller scale. Cisco Systems, for example, typically evaluates three potential markets for each one it decides to enter and then takes a hard look at five to ten candidates for each deal it does. Assessing a large volume of opportunities confers two main benefits. It gives Cisco an overall sense of what kinds of strategic acquisition opportunities exist and at what price, making the company better able to assess the value of each prospect relative to the others. On a more basic level, it forces managers to bring discipline and speed to the screening process.

Keep a Strategic Focus

A common mistake for novice acquirers is to cast strategy aside in the face of an exciting opportunity. "The failure starts right at the beginning," one senior financial professional explained to us. "Someone at the top falls in love, and the word comes down, 'We are going to do that deal.' Once the decision gets made, the guys doing the deal just want to get it done. They start stretching the operating assumptions to make it work." Senior executives at LBO firms, however, are strict about sticking to guidelines. Joe Nolan, a partner at GTCR Golder Rauner, is very clear about his firm's focus: "We look for businesses where acquisition will be a core part of the growth strategy. We back people who know how to both operate and acquire companies, which is a rare combination. We invest in service companies and not manufacturing."

From Talking to Planning

Initial negotiations can take place in a variety of ways. Some cases occur through a structured process, such as an auction; others happen less formally through conversations between senior executives. Either way, the challenge at this second stage is for the senior management of both companies to agree that the potential for a deal is sufficient to justify investing resources in further exploration. Successful friendly acquirers follow much the same rules of thumb in nursing potential transactions through this phase.

Don't Get Bogged Down Over Price

It is usually unwise to try to establish a firm agreement on price this early. The parties simply don't have enough information. As Bob End, one of the founding partners at Stonington Partners, puts it: "You have to do some preliminary feeling out, but if you focus on price at the beginning, you are setting yourself up for failure. People start staking out positions and end up souring on the deal. I'd rather get some momentum around the business possibilities, to get people nodding their heads."

Identify Must-Haves

Although acquirers cannot afford to get tied up with too much detail at this stage, it is essential to pin down certain issues. Many of these are driven by the acquisition's

Managing the Deal Team

NO TEAM CAN MAKE a bad deal good, but a bad team can make a good deal bad. The challenges of managing a deal team are, in essence, much the same as those of any large project: how can you bring a large team with a variety of skills and agendas together to quickly achieve an objective that not everyone may agree with? It's a task familiar to any film production company, and experienced acquirers go about it in much the same way.

Use the same principal actors

While each deal involves a large total cast, deal teams at successful organizations such as Cypress and Cisco always have at their core a small group of people who have worked together in the past. They are then supplemented by inside and outside experts. Having an inner circle of people who are familiar with one another facilitates coordination and communication. It also grants the team a certain amount of emotional resilience in what can be an unsettling experience. "We are nine senior professionals, and all of us have worked together for at least a decade," explains Cypress vice chairman Jeff Hughes. "That's long enough that everyone knows it's not personal if a deal gets killed. We all succeed or fail together." All transactions must have a clear leader and, although deal managers often start as a deal's advocate, they must be prepared to kill the deal if necessary.

Explain the plot

Team members have to talk to one another, of course, particularly during due diligence. As obvious as this advice might be, it can often be overlooked even though communication can be encouraged by fairly simple formal means, such as placing the working groups in a bullpen environment. Some of the most experienced acquirers require their teams to conduct daily roundtable discussions, so that everyone can hear the progress, the issues, and the concerns of the rest of the team. The deal managers encourage team members to contribute to these meetings and take care to discourage any hoarding of information.

strategic rationale. GTCR Golder Rauner, for example, focuses on the management team's experience and its incentive structure. Cisco insists that the management of target companies believes in employee ownership. It's also important to clarify the roles that the target's top executives will play in the combined organization: who will be retained, and what will they do? American Home Products' merger with Monsanto foundered, for example, because the two CEOs could not agree on which of them would be number one. Finally, it is essential that the acquirer be comfortable at this stage with any potential liabilities—such as environmental exposures, retiree health-care liabilities, or class action suits—that could materially affect the price of the transaction.

Get Friendly
It's only natural that the management team of a target company going into preliminary negotiations should feel nervous, even suspicious, of potential new owners. Savvy acquirers use early negotiations to foster a sense that both sides are working together in good faith to arrive at a mutually advantageous transaction. They are flexible and respectful in their negotiations, and they try to help target managers see the career opportunities that could result in the new organization. Says Jeff Hughes, vice chairman of the Cypress Group: "We build relationships with partners. It's how we approach deals from the very beginning, from the first meeting. You can't get a deal done unless you understand what the seller wants. You always have to solve people's problems." It's important to build "relationship capital" early on because it

will be needed in the later stages of the deal. As the acquisition moves through due diligence, final agreement, and closure, the acquirer's deal team will inevitably become much more assertive and demanding.

Gearing Up for Negotiations

The next stage, due diligence, is the most time consuming and least creative part of the process: the deal goes from the high romance of partnership to the mundane world of fact checking. Unsurprisingly, the eyes of many senior managers tend to glaze over at the prospect, and they leave the job to business development staff, line managers, accountants, lawyers, and bankers. But that boredom is dangerous: acquirers have wiped more value off their market capitalization through failures in due diligence than through lapses in any other part of the deal process. Smart acquirers approach a $1 billion acquisition with the same attention to detail they would apply to investing $1 billion in building a new plant.

Turn Over All the Rocks

In the excitement of the moment, the novice acquirer may be distracted from looking too closely at the details. That's a mistake because a deal that dies at the due diligence stage almost always dies for the right reasons. Recently, a prospective buyer was conducting diligence on a rapidly growing development-stage consumer service company with a robust product that dominated its niche. Initial assessments were highly favorable, but a deeper look revealed that the visionary founder had not put in place an adequate financial control system. The target's profitability was illusory, and the buyer abandoned the transaction. Hidden problems of this type are about more than money—they also raise important concerns about the competence, even honesty, of the target's management team.

Size Up the Other Side

Experienced acquirers use due diligence to deepen their knowledge about—and links with—the target's management. Every such interaction offers acquirers a priceless opportunity to assess people's abilities and personal agendas. Do the target's managers have command of their company's operational details? Do they work well as a team? Are they easily flustered or hostile when challenged? Are they enthused by the transaction, or are they more concerned about their personal futures? In due diligence for a recent media deal, for instance, it became clear to the acquirer that the target's founder and owner had certain priorities and motives for the deal, including a desire for a major role in the combined entity. Using that knowledge, the acquirer was able to structure a deal that satisfied the founder's aspirations to such an extent that he was willing to make significant concessions on price.

Feed Due Diligence into Business Planning

For novice acquirers, the due diligence process is just an information-gathering exercise, a break between initial and final negotiations. They usually do not begin to formulate strategy or build a valuation model until the process is complete. In some cases, different people conduct due diligence and final negotiations. Experienced acquirers, however, link their due diligence closely to business planning. Stonington Partners, for example, puts together a book on each acquisition, covering the investment thesis, the business model, capital structure, a base case valuation, a sensitivity analysis, and third-party due diligence. Stonington also keeps the original deal team involved throughout the process.

Getting to Final Terms

The fourth phase of the deal, in which the management teams of both sides and their advisers conduct negotiations on price and strategy, is the most sensitive. A typical mistake for novice teams at this stage is to come to the table with a large list of outstanding issues, which they then try to resolve in no particular order. The danger of this approach is that talks will get stalled on relatively trivial items, exhausting the hard-won goodwill gained in earlier stages and affording openings for rival bidders. Experienced acquirers are conscious of the need to maintain the momentum of the talks, and they are always aware of external threats.

Use Multiple Negotiation Channels
Senior managers, who may have steered the process to this point, often take the view that their company needs to speak with one clear voice at the negotiating table, and therefore they limit the negotiating team to a few

Managing the Deal Cycle

THE NEGOTIATION OF EVERY deal goes through five distinct phases, and for each phase, experienced serial acquirers strictly adhere to several negotiating principles:

1. Screening Potential Deals

- Look at all potential deals in your market, not just at the deal at hand.
- Don't cast strategy aside in the face of an exciting opportunity.

2. Reaching Initial Agreement

- Don't focus on price yet.
- Identify the details critical to the deal's success.
- Use early negotiations to foster a sense of trust with the target's top executives.

3. Conducting Due Diligence

- Look for the devil in the details.
- Deepen your understanding of the target's operating managers.
- Link due diligence with business planning.

4. Setting Final Terms

- Negotiate on several fronts simultaneously.
- Make sure you have alternatives to this deal.
- Anticipate the competition.

5. Achieving Closure

- Oversell to stakeholders.
- Close quickly after setting final terms.

key people. We strongly disagree with this approach. Successful acquirers usually divide their deal team into two or three separate negotiating groups: managers, lawyers, and perhaps investment bankers.

This division of labor has a number of important benefits. For one, it allows for parallel processing. The legal teams can, for example, make significant progress on the acquisition agreement while the bankers address the terms and structure of the financing. The managers, meanwhile, can focus on strategic and personnel issues, stepping into the other negotiations only to overcome impasses. Negotiating through multiple channels also makes it easier to send informal messages. An acquirer's management team may, for example, insist that the major selling shareholder sign a noncompetition agreement. At the same time, however, without conceding this point, the acquirer's investment banker or lawyer could hold hypothetical conversations about different ways to address the same concern. Finally, negotiation at different levels isolates acrimony. The principals can use the bankers and lawyers to deliver hard messages or to take inflexible positions without poisoning relationships with their counterparts.

Cultivate Alternatives
When an opportunity goes live, some deal managers focus on it to the exclusion of other opportunities. That's a natural instinct given constraints on managers' time. Nevertheless, we believe acquirers should carry on as vigorous a dialogue as possible with alternative targets. The value of understanding your best alternative to

negotiated agreement (or BATNA) has been well explored in popular books on negotiation, such as Roger Fisher, William Ury, and Bruce Patton's *Getting to Yes* (Houghton-Mifflin, 1992). Knowing what the alternatives are makes it easier to judge the relative value of the deal at hand and can shift the balance of power between acquirer and target. In a recent acquisition of a telecommunications company, for example, the acquirer was able to announce in the middle of negotiations that it had agreed to buy another, related company, significantly reducing its need for the first target. An acquirer's deal team behaves more confidently when it knows it has a choice—and that confidence gets projected across the table.

Anticipate the Competition

In most acquisitions, the target has a choice, and negotiations may even be taking place in the context of a structured auction. Before deciding on tactics, therefore, acquirers should assess their advantages and disadvantages relative to other potential bidders. (For a list of the key points to consider when comparing your company with potential competitors, see the sidebar "Are You the Strongest Acquirer?") That assessment should include a calculation of the long-term cost of losing the opportunity to a competitor. In some cases, an acquirer may want to avoid that situation by making a pre-emptive initial bid. IBM's unsolicited bid for Lotus Development, for example, was made at twice the target's prebid stock price.

In general, however, experienced acquirers avoid such tactics. Indeed, some financial acquirers have a strict policy of not participating in competitive auctions

Are You the Strongest Acquirer?

IN COMPETITIVE BIDDING SITUATIONS, an acquirer should compare its position with its rivals' along the following dimensions:

- ability to realize synergies with the target
- financing capacity
- ability to make quick decisions
- attractiveness of currency, in the case of stock-for-stock acquisitions
- reputation for getting deals done
- reputation for treating target's management with respect and for successfully integrating target's management

---

because they're convinced that the winner is often the party that overpaid. For the same reason, many corporate acquirers, like Cisco, also insist that substantive conversations be carried out on an exclusive basis.

Making It Happen

Once the ink on the final agreement has dried, it's easy for managers to think that the deal is done, but a surprising number of deals fall apart between final agreement and closure, the last stage of the process. There are sometimes very good reasons for that to happen—an environmental disaster may happen, some undisclosed liability may become apparent, or some adverse change in the target's competitive position may occur. (For instance, in 1998, Tellab's acquisition of telecom equipment maker Ciena fell apart when Ciena lost two key contracts after the final agreement was reached.) But a lot of deals fail at this point because acquirers do not take the trouble to sell the deal to key stakeholders or because they allow too much time to elapse between agreement and closure.

Sell, Sell, Sell

It's understandably hard for management, at the end of an exhausting negotiation, to shift quickly to the task of enthusiastically selling a deal to stakeholders. But in many cases, the final agreement is the first time investors get to voice their opinion on the deal, and their reactions can torpedo it. Earlier this year IMS Health, a major health care information provider, agreed to merge with TriZetto Group, an Internet health care company. The market reaction was immediate and negative—investors wiped some $2 bilion off the companies' combined market capitalization. The press noted at the time that a "lack of details surrounding the deal caused the shake-up in the stocks." A major shareholder subsequently released a letter to the company noting management's "inept" performance on an analyst conference call. The transaction was subsequently restructured as merely a sale of an IMS division to TriZetto.

Smart acquirers, therefore, are swift to follow their final deal agreements with aggressive and carefully planned public relations and investor relations campaigns, often involving professional PR advisers. Full and clear disclosure of the terms and the rationale for the deal is key. As Ammar Hanafi, vice president of business development at Cisco Systems, puts it: "I tend to over-communicate. The Street has to understand the strategy and how the acquisition fits in."

Nor can any corporation afford to neglect its key internal constituencies, as Deutsche Bank's CEO Rolf Breuer learned to his cost earlier this year from Deutsche's failed merger with rival Dresdner Bank. His mixed signals about the future of the combined organization's investment-banking operations outraged investment bankers in both camps, ultimately scuppering a deal that would have created a global force in banking.

Move Fast

However aggressively the CEOs and managers have sold the deal, not everyone will be happy with it. The target's line employees in particular will be worried about adapting to a different operating culture. In some cases, they will have legitimate concerns for their job security. At the same time, the target's customers will be wondering whether the acquirer will damage long-established relationships. Savvy acquirers keep the time between signing and closing as short as possible—ideally, to less than three months. They realize that quick closure gives them a better chance of showing the target's employees and customers that the deal will work. As Steve Holtzman, chief business officer at Millennium Pharmaceuticals, expresses it: "Time is your enemy. Once you have the idea, and you are agreed, then get it done. You can't go in and slam the deal together necessarily very quickly; you may need an up-front courting process. But once the courting is done, nail it." What's more, a prompt closure provides a

Postmortem Questions

WHETHER A DEAL SUCCEEDS or fails determines which questions to ask when trying to glean lessons learned. In both cases, the questions are straightforward, but the answers are invaluable.

What to Ask After a Failed Deal

- Was missing this acquisition a win or a loss for the company?

- If it was a loss, what could we have done differently?

- If it was a win, what did we do well that kept us out of this transaction?

- How could we have spotted the flaws earlier and spent less time on this opportunity?

What to Ask After a Successful Deal

- What did we do well in the process?

- What problems did we miss and when?

- How can we improve our process to uncover those problems earlier?

- How does what we bought compare with what we thought we were buying?

signal to key constituents—including investors—that the acquirer's managers know what they're doing.

Learning from Experience

All too often, the expensive lessons that acquirers learn are forgotten once the deal is over. But LBO shops constantly refine their approach; they treat every deal—even the missed opportunities—as a learning experience. Says GTCR Golder Rauner's Nolan: "If we passed on a deal and it succeeded, we'll revisit why we let it go. If we do something and it doesn't work out the way we

Ispat: A Great Corporate Acquirer

ALTHOUGH THE MAJORITY OF corporate acquirers have a poor track record, a few have successfully pursued long-term acquisition strategies. One such company is steelmaker Ispat International.

Ispat (which is Sanskrit for "steel") is one of the world's largest steel companies. This growth has come almost entirely through a decade-long series of acquisitions, starting with the purchase in 1988 of Trinidad and Tobago's state steel companies, and culminating with the purchase of Unimétal, Tréfileurope, and Société Métallurgique de Révigny from the French steel giant Usinor.

What's interesting about Ispat is that its M&A activities are organized very much like those of an LBO shop. To start with, Ispat's acquisitions are strictly focused. As president and COO Johannes Sittard explains: "While our expertise could be used in other industries, we never go outside our core business. So we understand the candidates and have a clear vision for where they could fit."

Once an opportunity has been selected, Ispat sends a small team to visit the seller. Here Ispat tries to gauge the seller's expectations and see if purchasing the assets makes sense. One of the key must-haves for a transaction to proceed to the next stage is that the target demonstrate that its labor supply and access to electricity are solid.

expected, we sit down and figure out the lessons learned. We also try to pass those lessons on to the executives we've been working with."

In our experience, it's wise to postpone a detailed analysis of a deal for at least a month—especially if there have been problems. In the aftermath of a failed deal, team members will be disappointed and may well channel their energies into a hunt for blame. With the benefit of further information, though (including the subsequent performance of the target), the lessons should

Ispat's due diligence process, which has been honed over time, focuses not just on gathering facts but, as Sittard observes, "We use due diligence to learn about the people who are running the company and to convince them that joining Ispat is an opportunity for them to grow. These conversations provide information you will never find in a data room."

The company works with the potential acquisition's management to develop a five-year business plan that will not only provide an acceptable return on investment but will also chime with Ispat's overall strategy. Ispat's managers know that they may end up responsible for managing the target, and that helps discourage them from making unrealistic assumptions about its prospects.

Ispat relies on a core team of just 12 to 14 professionals to manage its acquisitions. Based in London, the team's members all have solid operational backgrounds and have worked together since 1991. To support the team, Ispat draws in additional experts from its operating units as needed. The company learns from its experiences. "We are a small team, and acquisitions are much of what we do," Sittard explains, "so postacquisition assessments are a permanent part of our conversations."

become clearer and may often turn out to be quite different from initial impressions. The first postmortem session should therefore be brief, focusing primarily on setting an agenda and a time for holding the later meeting. And fixing that agenda should not be very difficult to do because, as you can see from the sidebar "Postmortem Questions," the key issues are fairly obvious, although which questions need to be posed depends on whether or not the deal was a success.

As successful acquirers have found, effective deal management is a source of sustainable competitive advantage, especially in rapidly growing or consolidating industries. Companies that can't close deals and are known to be dysfunctional negotiators will have fewer opportunities and will soon be outgrown by their more acquisitive competitors. Conversely, companies that effectively execute an acquisition strategy can vault to leadership positions in their industries. A case in point is Ispat International, a corporate acquirer that conducts its M&A activities very much as an LBO shop does. Twelve years ago, Ispat was a little-known Indian steel company with a single mill in Indonesia. Today, thanks to a series of well-managed and well-timed acquisitions, it is one of the world's leading steel companies. (For the story behind Ispat's success, see the sidebar "Ispat: A Great Corporate Acquirer.")

Following the operating principles we've described will certainly help companies become better acquirers. And they will become even better if they learn how to learn. But there will always be some element of art to deal making. Mastery of the art of acquisition can be achieved only through experience.

Note

1. The study that turned up the surprising statistic was published in a 1996 article in *The McKinsey Quarterly* entitled "Growth Through Acquisitions: A Fresh Look," by P. L. Anslinger and T. E. Copeland.

ROBERT J. AIELLO is a managing director and a cohead of the Technology Mergers and Acquisitions Group at

Prudential Securities. **MICHAEL D. WATKINS** is an associate professor at Harvard Business School.

Originally published in December 2000. Reprint R00602

Negotiating the Spirit of the Deal

by Ron S. Fortgang, David A. Lax, and James K. Sebenius

EXPERIENCED NEGOTIATORS ARE generally comfortable working out the terms of an economic contract: They bargain for the best price, haggle over equity splits, and iron out detailed exit clauses. But these same seasoned professionals often spend so much time hammering out the letter of the deal that they pay little attention to the social contract, or the spirit of the deal. So while the parties agree to the same terms on paper, they may actually have very different expectations about how the agreement will work in practice. Without their arriving at a true meeting of the minds, the deal they've signed may sour.

Consider the fate of a joint venture launched by two chains: a national hospital organization and a regional health care provider. Executives at these organizations realized that two of their hospitals, located near each other, were competing for doctors' practices and building redundant facilities. In response, they enthusiastically negotiated a joint venture that would manage the two hospitals and buy or build needed facilities within their shared area.

The two partners created a governance system and appointed managers to whom they offered incentives to maximize the venture's profits. Yet despite compelling economics, the arrangement didn't last—largely because the partners held clashing but unspoken assumptions about the joint venture's purpose. Moreover, the contract they actually negotiated didn't fit either organization's real objective.

Because the national chain had only one hospital in the region, it resisted economically sensible steps, like eliminating redundant departments, which were consistent with the joint venture's formal contract and management incentives. The national chain was understandably concerned that the joint venture might one day fail and its hospital—now offering reduced services—would no longer be competitive. Executives at the regional chain, by contrast, saw the joint venture as a way to extend and rationalize their regional network. They persisted in trying to make the regional operation more efficient, but the formal contract and management incentives—to maximize only the joint venture's profits—conflicted with that mission, too. Had the parties better understood each other's views of the underlying purpose of the venture in the first place, they might have forged a more limited, but more effective, agreement. Such a deal would have ignored possible operating efficiencies and focused on gains from jointly buying practices and building shared feeder facilities. As it happened, each organization's underlying

Idea in Brief

The deal looked so promising: a merger of Deutsche Bank and Dresdner, which would have produced the world's third largest bank. But the agreement unraveled within hours of its announcement.

What happened? While the parties had agreed to the *letter* of the deal—the economic contract—they neglected its *spirit*—the **social contract**—which included assumptions that the new entity wouldn't sell a Dresdner division.

Though parties may agree to identical terms on paper, they may have contrasting expectations about how their agreement will work *in practice*. Unless they concur on the social contract—that is, by explicitly discussing assumptions *before* cementing a deal—the agreement may sour.

expectations clashed both with the other's and with the actual contract, transforming enthusiasm and potential profits into a swamp of recriminations.

Based on our participation in hundreds of negotiations and a growing body of academic work on implicit and "relational" contracts, we have come to believe that cultivating a shared understanding of the spirit of the deal can be every bit as important as agreeing on the letter of the deal.[1] This article explains what the social contract is, shows how the parties' views of the social contract can sharply diverge, explores problems that arise when the social and economic contracts are at odds, and suggests ways to negotiate both so that they are independently strong as well as mutually reinforcing.

The Underlying Social Contract

The term "social contract" carries political connotations, bringing to mind the writings of Locke and Rousseau, but

Idea in Practice

The Social Contract

The social contract has two levels:

- **The underlying social contract** answers, *What* is our agreement's nature and purpose? Is this a short- or long-term deal? A discrete transaction or partnership? How much autonomy will each party have? What decisions will each participate in? Parties differing in basic ways—small versus large, entrepreneurial versus bureaucratic, and so on—often hold divergent views of the underlying social contract.

- **The ongoing social contract** answers, *How* will we work together? How will we communicate? Consult with each other? Resolve disputes? Handle surprises?

Risk Factors

Lack of awareness causes most social-contract misunderstandings. Parties form expectations about how the deal will be implemented but don't necessarily discuss them. Certain conditions are especially ripe for misunderstandings:

- **Cultures clash.** When a U.S. plant manager instigated downsizing at NCR Japan, differing cultural expectations about lifetime employment sparked organization of a union and a supplier boycott at NCR Japan.

- **Third parties drive the deal.** When investment bankers or other professional negotiators drive deals, conflicting social-contract assumptions can be overlooked. Involve those who must make the deal work in the negotiating process—where they can begin forging a positive social contract.

  Example: When Matsushita Electric considered acquiring MCA (owner of movie studios and record companies),

we use the concept on a radically smaller scale. In a negotiation context, we define the social contract in terms of the parties' expectations. This contract has two levels: The *underlying social contract* answers the question, What? (For instance, are we working out a series of former talent agent Michael Ovitz brokered the deal. To build momentum, Ovitz *separated* the parties during negotiation—unwittingly causing each side to form distorted views of the other's intentions. Result? Post-deal friction and Matsushita's sale of MCA to Seagram several years later—at a $1.64 billion loss.

- **Too few parties are involved in the deal.** Even tightly aligned social and economic contracts can fragment if only a few individuals share the agreement's expectations. Widen the web of dependencies throughout your company to cultivate more sustainable relationships—and greater commitment to implementing agreements.

Dovetailing the Contracts

To boost your deal's chances of success, make economic and social contracts mutually reinforcing.

Example: To save its business in the late 1980s, Chrysler defined a new *social* contract emphasizing cooperation and long-term partnerships with suppliers, expecting them to improve their own performance *and* enhance Chrysler's overall operations. It also revised its *economic* contracts. Rather than selecting lowest bidders, it prequalified suppliers based on their engineering and manufacturing capabilities and past performance, then lengthened contract life from two to four years. The payoff? A 32% reduction in vehicle-development time and rise in per-vehicle profit from $250 to $2,110.

discrete transactions or a real partnership? *What* is the real nature, extent, and duration of our agreement?) The *ongoing social contract* answers the question, How? (In practice, *how* will we make decisions, handle unforeseen events, communicate, and resolve disputes?)

We'll look at the underlying social contract first. Too many negotiators leave the underlying social contract implicit, which can cause misunderstandings and ultimately poison a relationship. Rather than discuss their expectations during negotiations, the parties project their own reasonable, but sometimes incompatible, assumptions about the fundamental nature of the deal. Some people, for instance, view a contract as a starting point for a problem-solving relationship. Dan Orum, the president of Online Operations at Oxygen Media, is in that camp. He says, "The five words I most hate to hear in my business dealings [are], 'It's not in the contract.'" If the person he is negotiating with takes a more legalistic approach and sees the contract as an exhaustive description of mutual obligations, issues are bound to arise. That's why parties should strive for a real meeting of the minds on whether they are entering a problem-solving partnership or simply making a series of discrete transactions. Each approach is valid; the important thing is to recognize the potential for differing views and to try to align them.

Like clashing views of partnership versus transaction, divergent assumptions about autonomy versus conformity may create problems when the difference is identified late in the game. Consider what happened to an entrepreneur who failed to get clarity on this issue before she sold her boutique enterprise to a very eager corporate buyer. She decided to sell and agreed to stay on for five years because the purchaser assured her that she was "the essential player to lead the business to the next level" and because she envisioned her still-autonomous unit turbocharged by the acquirer's size, reach, and resources. The responsible corporate executive passionately shared her goal of taking the boutique concept global, but he simply assumed that only by following highly disciplined corporate procedures would the global rollout be possible.

Soon after the celebratory dinner, the unhappy reality began to dawn on the seller in the form of a legion of junior staff from HR delivering policy manuals and patronizing lectures on who bought whom. Even though the provisions of the economic contract—the letter of the deal on financial terms, governance, and the like— were acceptable to her, there had clearly been no meeting of the minds on the underlying social contract. Chances are, this will be one more failed acquisition despite its strategic logic, the skills and good intentions of both sides, and an acceptable economic contract.

Failure to make the underlying social contract explicit is by no means limited to small companies like the boutique enterprise. Take, for example, the proposed megamerger between Deutsche Bank and Dresdner, which would have produced the third-largest bank in the world (with $1.25 trillion in assets), leading many people to view the planned deal as a landmark in the transformation of Europe's financial services industry. The banks planned to merge their retail operations, enabling them to close about 700 branches and concentrate on their more profitable corporate businesses.

Throughout the negotiations, Deutsche chairman Rolf Breuer implied that this was to be a "merger of equals." Although the new bank was to bear Deutsche

Bank's name, the corporate color was to be Dresdner's green. Bernhard Walter, Dresdner's chairman, was particularly concerned that Deutsche would sell off Dresdner Kleinwort Benson (DrKB), which had contributed more than half of Dresdner's 1999 pretax profits. Aware of Dresdner's sensitivities, Breuer uttered words that would soon haunt him: "[DrKB] is a jewel, and we want to keep that jewel. It will be neither closed nor sold, and any reports to the contrary are 'barer Unsinn' [pure nonsense]." Satisfied, Walter declared, "A merger means you combine both parts into a new whole. I never had the slightest feeling that things would go differently."

Yet within hours of the joint announcement of the merger, Deutsche apparently decided to sell DrKB, believing that its own investment-banking arm had further global reach. And by selling the unit, Breuer wouldn't have to go through the long and expensive process of integrating DrKB's 7,500 employees. When DrKB staff members learned of this decision (from a *Financial Times* article by a source who came to be called the "torchman"), they moved to a state of alert.[2] The report mobilized powerful internal opponents to block the deal. In light of this clash—together with growing investor doubts about the deal's business rationale and actual terms—the merger was called off, after a month of furious negotiations, protestations of misunderstanding, and efforts at compromise. During that time, Deutsche's share price plunged 19%, and Dresdner's fell almost as much. Whether by accident or design, Deutsche's vision of the underlying social contract was at odds with Dresdner's, and those opposing assumptions helped to doom the deal.

Parties that differ in basic ways are especially likely to hold divergent views of the underlying social contract. Such differences could involve the companies' size, organizational approach, and business focus: small versus large, entrepreneurial versus bureaucratic, centrally managed versus decentralized, and finance driven versus operations centered. For example, serious postalliance ownership conflict between Northwest Airlines and KLM Royal Dutch Airlines was less due to a cultural clash than it was exacerbated by a disagreement over management focus and risk tolerance. Pieter Bouw, KLM's Dutch president, stressed airline operations and conservative financial management. Gary Wilson and Al Checchi were high-profile, risk-taking financiers who had acquired Northwest in a highly leveraged buyout. Even agreement on the terms of an economic contract could not resolve those fundamentally different approaches to running an airline.

The examples given thus far illustrate some of the issues that need to be aired about whether minds have truly met on the underlying social contract. Other questions include, Is this a short- or long-term deal? Is it openended or task specific? Will it be learning or production oriented? Do we believe in lifetime or at-will employment? In countless deals, the tangible terms may seem fine, but the two sides realize only when it's too late that the reality doesn't match their expectations.

Although agreeing on the underlying social contract is important, a degree of what diplomats call "constructive ambiguity" is sometimes appropriate. Imagine, for example, two companies that both want control in a proposed equity joint venture. If pressed to fully resolve the issue at the outset, they would probably walk away from the deal. Yet if they could agree to launch a pilot venture with shared control, even if each side still believes that it must have total control in the ultimate venture, the deal might build their confidence in their ability to work together—even without such control. Success in the pilot could change the way they approach the social contract in the larger deal. As the French saying goes, "There could be no treaties without conflicting mental reservations." The trick, of course, is to distinguish true confidence-building steps from the papering over of fatal differences.

The Ongoing Social Contract

Just as important as the underlying social contract is the ongoing social contract. It answers the question, How will we work together? Properly negotiated, it outlines the broad process expectations for how the parties will interact: norms for communication, consultation, and decision making; how unforeseen events will be handled; dispute resolution; conditions and means for renegotiation; and the like.

A positive ongoing social contract can foster efficient sharing of information; lower the costs of complex adaptation; permit rapid exploitation of unexpected opportunities without the parties having to write, monitor, and enforce complete contracts; and reduce transaction costs and even fears of exploitation. In fact, in a 1997 study of North American and Asian automakers and suppliers, then Wharton professor Jeffrey Dyer found that "General Motors procurement (transaction) costs were more than twice those of Chrysler's and six times higher than Toyota's. GM's transaction costs are persistently higher . . . because suppliers view GM as a much less trustworthy organization."

Clearly, a well-functioning ongoing social contract is beneficial, but too often, partners hold conflicting expectations. Imagine, for example, that a global manufacturer has a joint venture with a major local distributor. The relationship runs smoothly until the manufacturer approaches another distributor about selling a different product line. Since the economic contract governing their joint venture said nothing about the new line, the manufacturer may think it perfectly reasonable to use another distributor. But the first distributor may have expected to have been given the opportunity and may think that the manufacturer has acted in bad faith. Because their assumptions were never made clear, their relationship suffers, even though no actual breach of contract has occurred.

Because conscious efforts to shape the social contract can help stave off problems like this, we suggest that both sides conduct an audit of sorts. They should formally ask such straightforward questions as, How will we handle proprietary information? About what actions—inside and outside the bounds of the deal—will we inform each other? How do we properly launch a partnership? (For more on questions to ask in an audit, see the sidebar "Conducting an Audit: Sample Questions.")

A final note on forging a productive ongoing social contract: It is often beneficial for senior executives to be involved in every stage of the deal. Ford and Mazda did an excellent job at this. In 1969, the automakers began a remarkable strategic partnership, initially driven by Ford's search for a low-cost production source and Mazda's desire to break into the U.S. market. Serious disputes erupted because of U.S.—Japanese political tensions, efforts to protect proprietary technology, cultural differences, product design, and material selection. To deal with these problems, senior executives (three top managers from Ford and Mazda and six other operating heads) held a three-day summit every eight months. The first two days of these summits were devoted to strategy and operations, but the third typically functioned to repair or realign the social contract as needed.

Risk Factors

The most common causes of social contract problems are lack of awareness and benign neglect. The parties involved inevitably form expectations about how the deal will be carried out, whether they discuss them or not. Even if initially compatible, those expectations can silently shift in response to actions taken, even though no overt negotiation takes place. Of course, if costly misunderstandings are to be avoided, it's normally in the parties' best interests to make their expectations explicit and negotiable. And red flags should go up when especially challenging conditions, such as the following, are present.

When Cultures Clash

Negotiators from diverse organizational, professional, or national cultures often bring clashing assumptions to the table. As Ming-Jer Chen, the former director of Wharton's Global Chinese Business Initiative, explains in *Inside Chinese Business,* "The Chinese perceive contracts as too rigid to take new circumstances into account. Hence, there is no stigma to changing the terms of an agreement after it has been signed." That approach often frustrates businesspeople who assume a signed contract is a done deal and a complete, fixed description of each side's obligations.

Consider how cultural expectations damaged relationships at NCR Japan. While the company was U.S. owned, it had a history of stable lifetime employment and a union that enjoyed close relations with management. However, when the plant's first U.S. manager instigated downsizing to enhance returns—even though the plant was profitable—employees resisted this perceived violation of the underlying social contract. A second union was quickly organized, and it took a far more adversarial approach, demanding higher wages and insisting on job guarantees. Local suppliers saw the company as untrustworthy and refused to do business with it. A full decade after the plant manager was ousted, the second union remained in power, and the supplier boycott continued.

Conducting an Audit

Sample Questions

Discussing expectations *before* you sign a deal can greatly increase the odds of its success. To help you get that conversation started, here are some sample questions about the letter and spirit of your deal.

Underlying Social Contract

Real nature and purpose of the agreement. Do you envision a discrete transaction or a partnership? A merger of equals or something quite different? Are you building an institution for the long term or making a financial investment with a nearer horizon? What is the driving culture (operational, for example, or research oriented)?

Scope and duration. Is your agreement focused on a discrete, short-term task, or is it open-ended? Is it a likely prelude to a larger or different arrangement? What kinds of actions, even outside the bounds of the deal, do you expect to be told about? And about which do you expect some say?

Ongoing Social Contract

Consultation. How fully, formally, and frequently do you expect to consult with the other side? How extensively will you and your partner share or protect information?

This example underscores not only the risk of underestimating differences between cultures but also the strength of the backlash to perceived breaches of a social contract. It's important to note here that not all breaches need be fatal; how they are handled can strengthen or rupture the social contract. If a breach is inadvertent, for example, managers normally should acknowledge it and reassure the other side that the "violation" was unintentional, not exploitative. Indeed,

Decision making. Beyond the formal governance mechanisms, by what process do you want to discuss and make decisions: by consensus or majority? Informally or formally? Who will be involved?

Dispute resolution. In the case of conflict, what approach do you expect to use: informal discussion, mediation, binding arbitration, court? What if disagreement persists?

Reevaluation and renegotiation. How will you handle unexpected challenges (such as changing economics or competitive dynamics)? What should trigger reevaluation or renegotiation, and what should you and your partner expect from each other in such a case?

Meeting of the Minds and Fit

Alignment. Do the economic and social contracts reinforce each other? If they don't, what should you and your partner do to align them?

Shared perceptions. All things considered, what's your view of the social and economic contracts? What do others in your organization think? What is the other side's view, and does it mesh with yours? How do you know? How can you and your partner ensure that you have a real meeting of the minds on your perceptions? If you discover divergent perceptions, how should you resolve them?

---

sincere efforts to rebuild confidence can often buttress the existing social contract.

When the Wrong Minds Meet

Sometimes problems arise not because of cultural differences but instead because the right people are not involved in negotiations. For example, when two CEOs negotiate a strategic partnership—say between a retailer and a supplier—they may stress the importance of many dimensions of cooperation, the mutual need for service and quality, and the long-term time horizon of the joint effort. Yet the retail buyer, for instance—mainly compensated on the basis of quarterly numbers—refers to "our strategic partnership" primarily to beat price reductions out of the supplier. This problem will persist unless senior retail executives work to reset employees' expectations and incentives at the working level when they forge what *they* see as a strategic alliance.

There are other, less obvious, ways that key parties are inadvertently omitted from social contract negotiations. For example, in 1988, Komatsu, Japan's leader in earth-moving construction equipment, and U.S. conglomerate Dresser Industries combined their North American engineering, manufacturing, and marketing efforts to attain what they called a "mountain of treasure." Dresser sought Komatsu's design technology and a cash infusion for plant modernization and capital expenditures. Komatsu hoped to become a successful global player, so it wanted better North American market penetration. While preserving parallel brands and distributorships, Komatsu and Dresser created a 50-50 joint venture (Komatsu Dresser Corporation, or KDC), merging manufacturing, engineering, and finance operations. The joint venture maintained equal management representation on the six-person oversight committee and agreed to a $200 million investment. Beyond the economic terms of the companies' arrangement, they aimed to foster a strong social contract between their management teams.

Yet the implementation of their arrangement strained the emerging deal, and the separate distributors, who never subscribed to the new expectations, began competing for sales. Tensions escalated: Komatsu saw Dresser as backward and unresponsive; Dresser complained of learning about key Komatsu decisions after the fact. As the situation worsened, executives from both companies clamped down on communications, which prevented dealers from getting vital information about their counterpart's inventory levels and warranty coverage, further exacerbating the conflict.

Despite the efforts of industrial consultants and a last-minute plan to swap employees between the two companies, the dealer conflicts intensified, KDC market share declined sharply, losses mounted, 2,000 jobs were cut, and ultimately, the venture was dissolved. Subject to more than the usual cross-cultural hazards, KDC suffered: It failed to ensure that potentially influential parties bought into the new social contract.

When Third Parties Drive the Deal

Failure also happens when one team, such as the business development unit, uses a heavily price-driven process to negotiate an alliance or acquisition. Once the parties agree to the terms, the team "throws it over the fence" to operational management, which is stuck with the unenviable job of forging a strong, positive social contract after the fact. Jerry Kaplan, Go Technologies' founder, was especially critical of the negotiation process IBM used when it invested in Go. As Kaplan explains in *Startup,* "Rather than empowering the responsible party to make the deal, IBM assigns a professional negotiator, who knows or cares little for the substance of the agreement but has absolute authority." With a process like that, the right minds have little chance of truly meeting on the underlying social contract. It's almost always best to get the managers who must make the deal work involved in the negotiating process, where they can begin to forge a positive social contract.

In some cases, investment bankers or other deal makers with a powerful interest in making a transaction happen—for better or worse—can divert the principals' attention from possibly fatal differences in their views of the underlying social contract. For example, Matsushita Electric's primary rationale for paying $6.59 billion for MCA—owner of movie studios, record companies, and theme parks—was to ensure a steady flow of creative software for its global hardware businesses. Senior MCA management agreed to the acquisition, expecting the new, cash-rich Japanese parent to provide capital for acquiring more record companies, a television network, and so on, all of which were vital to helping the combined companies compete with rivals such as Disney and Cap Cities/ABC.

To get the deal done, however, Michael Ovitz, talent agent turned unorthodox corporate matchmaker, kept the parties mostly *apart* during the process, managing expectations separately on each side and building momentum until the deal was virtually closed. Neither side did its due diligence on their mutual perceptions of the real underlying social contract—partly because of the cultural chasms dividing old-line industrial Japan, creative Hollywood, and the New York financial community, but largely due to the deal-driving third party (Ovitz). As a result, each side had an optimistic but badly distorted view of the other's real intentions, leading to postdeal friction and the sale of MCA a few years later to Seagram, at a substantial loss to Matsushita both in financial terms (roughly $1.64 billion) and in prestige.

When Too Few Parties Are Involved in the Deal

Even a tightly aligned social and economic contract can be vulnerable if the expectations and agreements that underlie it are shared by only a select few. Senior partners in consulting firms, for instance, often depend primarily on their relationships with CEOs in their client companies. But if the CEO leaves, the consulting firm may lose the account. Consciously creating a wider web of involvements and dependencies throughout the firm would result in a more sustainable relationship—and greater commitment to implementation of agreed-upon recommendations—even when fewer participants could complete the consulting projects more efficiently.

Dovetailing the Contracts

It can be tempting to regard the social contract as unwritten and psychological and the economic contract as written and tangible. Yet the two can be productively dovetailed, with elements of the economic contract directly tied to the social one. Sometimes, the way to arrange such a fit seems obvious: A discrete, project-oriented agreement, for instance, should have clean, workable exit and termination provisions linked to both sides' understanding of when their shared objective is accomplished (or has become impossible). By contrast, if a deal's central aim is ongoing knowledge transfer, negotiators might set terms in the economic contract that would further that goal. For instance, when Wal-Mart and Procter & Gamble formed an alliance, interface team members signed confidentiality agreements, binding them from releasing information from team discussions even to their own parent companies. This cemented the group's commitment to total discretion and unleashed greater creativity, since members could try things out without fear that proprietary data would be shared outside the alliance team. Whatever the goal of the deal, it will generally be much easier to reach if the economic and social contracts are mutually reinforcing.

Some companies have mastered this skill. Italian apparel-maker Benetton, for example, has enjoyed many successes in new markets by following a tried-and-true formula. First, it establishes a local agent to develop licensees for products from Italy; then it develops local production capability, partnering with an area business for further market development. If that is successful, it buys out its partner, which typically retains a significant role, and integrates the foreign subsidiary into Benetton's global network. This staged approach has worked repeatedly because Benetton's contracts with its local partners explicitly detail the expected trajectory of the partnership and include formal mechanisms to accomplish its stated goal.

Many companies bungle the kind of smooth transitions Benetton often achieves because they fail to fully vet expectations about how their partnerships will run. If negotiations are handled poorly, high-status local partners can end up feeling betrayed and devalued by unexpected buyout initiatives. In addition, badly handled negotiations can result in unworkable valuation formulas that lead to disagreements, impasses, and the like. No successful private equity or venture capital firm would invest without establishing clear exit expectations for when milestones have been met or when circumstances have changed. Despite the potential awkwardness of negotiating a prenuptial agreement while heading into marriage, most companies should spell out similar provisions in their contracts.

To highlight how critical it is to dovetail the letter and spirit of a deal, we like to contrast two cases, negotiated by different experienced investors during the same year, in which subsequent attitudes toward the deal played key roles. The first involved prominent pediatricians who were looking for assistance to make a series of interactive CDs on parenting issues. A venture investor provided capital in return for a half-interest in the new company that would own all the doctors' products in this business area. The investor helped the doctors create a demo CD, wrote a business plan and marketing materials, and showed the entire package to key people at major software publishing houses. When a publisher expressed enthusiasm, the doctors surprised the investor by arguing that "he owned too much of the company," that "their ideas and reputation *were* the company," and that he should willingly reduce his stake. Needless to say, after all the time and effort he had invested in developing the company, he felt stung. When efforts at resolution reached an impasse, the new company languished, and the agreement blocked the doctors from developing their ideas elsewhere. Clearly, both sides neglected to work through different scenarios to test the perceived fairness and psychological sustainability of the deal, firm up their social contract, and alter the economics if necessary. As a result, great value was left unrealized.

By contrast, consider the contract a different investor designed when he was approached by a commercial banker who financed independent filmmakers. Although filmmaking is a risky business, the banker had not lost money on any of his 41 loans—in part because he had nurtured worldwide contacts and then presold foreign rights. Unhappy with his compensation as a bank employee, he was planning to leave and start a film-finance company. To get the fledgling business off the ground, he was seeking an $18 million investment to complement the $2 million he would contribute, and he offered the investor 90% of the new company.

Even though the investor's analysis projected a 100% annual rate of return on this investment, he turned down the offer and counterproposed a deal that was, in fact, more lucrative for the banker and less so for himself. The investor reasoned that in two or three years he would have simply taken the place of the bank, providing little but commodity capital, and the banker-entrepreneur would end up seeking a better deal from new capital sources. Therefore, his counteroffer contained a series of results-linked options: The banker would be able to buy back some of the investor's equity at a relatively low price after the investor had received his first $5 million, then buy back more equity after the investor had received the next $5 million, and so on. At each point under this deal structure, it would be in the banker's interest to stay in the relationship rather than to start out on his own again. The investor's projected rate of return on this offer was closer to 30%. But he preferred to sign a contract stipulating a 30% return that he believed he would actually receive rather than one with a 100% return on paper that would very likely spur the banker to abrogate at some point.

This investor understood that the spirit and letter of the deal needed to complement each other, whereas the investor who financed the doctors' CD development company struck an economically sensible but perhaps psychologically naive deal. The investor involved in the film-finance company structured his proposal to match predictable changes in circumstances and attitudes, and he found the right fit between the economic and social contracts.

Not only should the social contract complement the economic one, but the economic contract itself can also actually embody much of the social one. In the late 1980s, for example, Chrysler deliberately restructured both the letter and spirit of its contracts with suppliers to save its business. In 1989, the company faced a projected $1 billion overrun on a new program, a $4.5 billion unfunded pension liability, and a record loss of $664 million in the fourth quarter. To stop the hemorrhage, Chrysler decided to revolutionize its supplier relationships (along with other strategic measures). The automotive giant had traditionally given its business to the qualified bidder offering the lowest price, relying on supplier competition to drive down costs. Now it looked to form long-term partnerships with a subset of its traditional suppliers. In this new model, the partner was expected not only to improve its own performance but also to enhance Chrysler's operations beyond the supply relationship.

To support this new social contract, Chrysler substantially revised its economic contract. Rather than choosing the lowest price from qualified bidders, Chrysler prequalified a group of suppliers (1,140 out of its original 2,500) based on their advanced engineering and manufacturing capabilities and on their past performance in terms of on-time delivery and the like. Within this smaller set of players, Chrysler shifted from a system in which multiple suppliers competed over separate design, prototype, and production contracts to one in which a single supplier held primary responsibility for the combined design, prototype, and production of a component or system.

Under the old system, the average supplier contract lasted 2.1 years. The new approach saw the life of an average contract grow to 4.4 years, and Chrysler gave oral guarantees to more than 90% of its suppliers that the current business would remain with them for at least the life of the relevant model if performance targets were met. Because this new social contract stressed cooperation, Chrysler sought to ensure a fair profit for all parties. Instead of relying on commodity pricing to squeeze its suppliers, the automaker adopted a target-costing approach that worked backward from total cost to end user in order to calculate allowable costs for systems, subsystems, and components. Further, in keeping with the spirit of cooperation, Chrysler required suppliers to look beyond their own operations and find cost-saving possibilities within Chrysler itself equal to at least 5% of contract value—and suppliers would get half of the savings.

In essence, the written terms of the new economic contract—on selection, scope, duration, renewal, pricing, and performance requirements—consciously underpinned the new social contract emphasizing longer-term, integrated partnerships. The results were impressive: Chrysler was able to cut the time needed to develop a vehicle from an average of 234 weeks during the 1980s to 160 weeks in 1997—a 32% reduction. The cost of developing a vehicle plunged between 20% and 40% during the 1990s, and profit per vehicle jumped from an average of $250 during the late 1980s to a record of $2,110 in 1994. A new social contract deeply intertwined with the new economic one was largely responsible for these results.

Clearly, Chrysler saw dramatic improvements, but this particular social-economic contract combination isn't right for every company. Forging tight partnerships with a much smaller supplier base has some drawbacks.

These include the difficulty of further shrinking the supplier base as relationships deepen as well as the risk of being "held up" by a critical supplier that has no real competition, especially in a tough economy. The crucial point, however, is that the underlying and ongoing social contracts consist of more than purely "psychological" expectations; they can and should be embedded in and complemented by the formal economic contract.

Common Misperceptions

We have witnessed dozens of deals unravel or fall well short of their potential because the participants failed to achieve a meeting of the minds on the spirit of the deal. To avoid that fate, make sure you don't fall prey to the following misperceptions:

Many people believe that the social contract is primarily about the working relationship. But as we've shown, the social contract defines not just how the relationship will proceed but also exactly what the real nature of the relationship is. So while the ongoing social contract covers the working relationship—including expectations about communication, consultation, decision making, dispute resolution, and opportunities for renegotiation—the underlying social contract outlines expectations about the fundamental purpose, extent, and duration of the deal.

Another popular misconception is that the term "social contract" means a cooperative, democratic, and participatory relationship. The social contract can embody those ideals, but it need not. Indeed, a productive social contract could detail an autocratic relationship or an "eat what you kill" culture. What's key is that both parties move toward shared expectations about the deal.

Many people think that a social contract implies that the parties involved have a shared view. As we've shown, different parties can hold wildly divergent expectations about the deal, even when they've signed the same piece of paper. Reaching a shared understanding is crucial, but getting to that point takes focus and energy. A healthy social contract, mutually understood, is a goal, not a given.

Too many people set themselves up for failure because they think negotiation stops when the ink dries. However, even after the economic contract has been signed and minds have met on the underlying social contract, the parties should consider adapting the agreement to changed circumstances. And, by continuing to invest in the ongoing social contract, the people involved can help avoid costly misinterpretations and can greatly enhance the value of the economic contract, especially when they want to explore new opportunities or must tackle unexpected challenges.

A final misperception, and one that bears repeating, is that the social contract must be primarily psychological, or "soft"—not something that can be spelled out in a written agreement. But as we've shown, key provisions of the social contract—such as expectations about the nature and duration of the relationship—can often be made explicit in the economic contract. Negotiating complementary economic and social contracts greatly improves the odds that the deal will deliver the benefits it promises on paper.

Notes

The authors wish to thank Ashish Nanda, who provided invaluable insights and examples, as well as John Hammond, Rosabeth Moss Kanter, Deborah Kolb, Richard Meyer, Ken Mildwaters, Howard Raiffa, Jeff Weiss, Michael Yoshino, and members of the Harvard Negotiation Roundtable.

1. Sources for such studies, along with a more complete set of sources for this article, can be downloaded from http://www.people.hbs.edu/jsebenius/hbr/negotiating_the_spirit_of_the_deal_v3-41b.pdf.

2. "Torch That Sent a Deal Down in Flames," *Financial Times,* April 12, 2000.

RON S. FORTGANG, DAVID A. LAX, AND JAMES K. SEBENIUS are principals at Lax Sebenius, a negotiation-strategy consulting firm in Massachusetts. They are members of the Negotiation Roundtable forum at Harvard Business School.

Originally published in February 2003. Reprint RO302E

When to Walk Away from a Deal

by Geoffrey Cullinan, Jean-Marc Le Roux, and Rolf-Magnus Weddigen

DEAL MAKING IS GLAMOROUS; due diligence is not. That simple statement goes a long way toward explaining why so many companies have made so many acquisitions that have produced so little value. Although big companies often make a show of carefully analyzing the size and scope of a deal in question—assembling large teams and spending pots of money—the fact is, the momentum of the transaction is hard to resist once senior management has the target in its sights. Due diligence all too often becomes an exercise in verifying the target's financial statements rather than conducting a fair analysis of the deal's strategic logic and the acquirer's ability to realize value from it. Seldom does the process lead managers to kill potential acquisitions, even when the deals are deeply flawed.

Take the case of Safeway, a leading American grocery chain with a string of successful mergers to its credit and a highly respected management team. In 1998,

Safeway acquired Dominick's, an innovative regional grocer in the Chicago area. The strategic logic for the $1.8 billion deal seemed impeccable. It would add about 11% to Safeway's overall sales at a time when mass retailers like Wal-Mart and Kmart were stocking groceries on their shelves and taking market share away from established players, and it would give Safeway a strong presence in a major metropolitan market. Although Dominick's 7.5% operating cash flow margin lagged behind Safeway's 8.4%, Safeway CEO Steve Burd convinced investors that he would be able to quickly raise the acquired firm's margin to 9.5%. Capitalizing on this momentum, Safeway closed the deal in just five weeks, about a third of the average closing period for large acquisitions.

Safeway would come to regret not taking time for due diligence. Dominick's focus on prepared foods, in-store cafes, and product variety did not fit Safeway's emphasis on store brands and cost discipline. Dominick's strong unions resisted Safeway's aggressive cost-cutting plans. And with its customers unwilling to accept Safeway's private label goods, Dominick's was soon losing share to its archrival, Jewel. A thorough due diligence process would certainly have revealed these problems, and Safeway could have walked away with its pockets intact. Instead, it is stuck with an operation it cannot sell for even a fifth of the original purchase price.

Safeway is just one of many companies to suffer from weak due diligence. In December 2002, Bain & Company surveyed 250 international executives with M&A

Idea in Brief

Is your company prone to "deal fever"—getting so excited while pursuing acquisitions that it skimps on due diligence? Caught up in the thrill of the chase, many firms use due diligence to justify the deal rather than to uncover potentially serious problems.

To introduce discipline into your due diligence, Cullinan, Le Roux, and Weddigen recommend putting potential acquisitions' strategic rationale under the microscope: Probe for targets' strengths and weaknesses, and dig for unreliable assumptions. Be prepared to walk away.

Asking four questions can protect your company from ending up with a bad bargain:

- What are we *really* buying? (What would the acquisition bring, in terms of customers, competitors, costs, and capabilities?)

- What's the target's stand-alone value? (Your purchase price should reflect the target as it is, not as it might be once acquired.)

- Where are the synergies?

- What's the most we're willing to pay?

responsibilities. Half the participants said their due diligence processes had failed to uncover major problems, and half found that their targets had been dressed up to look better for the deals. Two-thirds said they routinely overestimated the synergies available from their acquisitions. Overall, only 30% of the executives were satisfied with the rigor of their due diligence processes. Fully a third admitted they hadn't walked away from deals they had nagging doubts about.

What can companies do to improve their due diligence? To answer that question, we've taken a close look at 20 companies—both public and private—whose

Idea in Practice

Cullinan, Le Roux, and Weddigen offer these guidelines for evaluating a potential acquisition:

What Are We *Really* Buying?

Instead of relying on information provided by the target company, build your own view of the target by gathering information on its:

- **Customers:** Who are the target's most profitable customers, and how well is it managing them? For example, how do its customers' profitability or vulnerability compare with those of the target's competitors?

- **Competition:** How does the target compare to rivals in terms of market share, revenues, and profits—by geography, product, and segment? How might its competitors react to the acquisition?

- **Costs:** Is the target performing above or below cost expectations given its relative market position? Why? What's the best cost position you could reasonably achieve by acquiring the target?

- **Capabilities:** What capabilities—management expertise, technologies, organizational structures—does the target have that create definable customer value?

What's the Target's Stand-Alone Value?

The vast majority of the price you pay for an acquisition should reflect the business as it is, not as it might be once you've won it. To determine stand-alone value, strip away tricks used by targets, such as stuffing distribution channels to inflate sales projections.

transactions have demonstrated high-quality due diligence. We calibrated our findings against our experiences in 2,000-odd deals we've screened over the past ten years. We've found that successful acquirers view due diligence as much more than an exercise in verifying data. While they go through the numbers deeply

WHEN TO WALK AWAY FROM A DEAL

Send a team into the field to see what's really happening with the target's costs and sales. If the target's hesitant or hostile about your investigation, steer clear.

Where Are the Synergies—and Dangers?

Assess the value of the acquisition's potential cost and revenue synergies by:

- **Estimating how long they'll take to achieve.** You can gain some synergies (such as eliminating duplicate functions) quickly. Others (such as selling new products through new channels) take much longer.

- **Assessing the probability of success.** Some synergies (such as combining facilities) have lower success rates because they involve complex personnel and regulatory issues.

- **Considering integration costs.** Anticipate post-acquisition events that can sap revenues or increase costs, such as defections of talented employees.

What's Our Walk-Away Price?

Your walk-away price is the top price you're willing to pay when the final negotiation is conducted. When establishing your walk-away price, give most weight to the current worth of the target company, and don't overestimate synergies' potential value—which may not materialize. Assemble a team of trusted individuals, less attached to the deal than senior management, who can provide an unbiased examination of the target and hold everyone to the walk-away criteria.

and thoroughly, they also put the broader, strategic rationale for their acquisitions under the microscope. They look at the business case in its entirety, probing for strengths and weaknesses and searching for unreliable assumptions and other flaws in the logic. They take a highly disciplined and objective approach to the process, and their senior executives pay close heed to the results of the investigations and analyses—to the extent that they are prepared to walk away from a deal, even in the very late stages of negotiations. For these companies, due diligence acts as a counterweight to the excitement that builds when managers begin to pursue a target.

The successful acquirers we studied were all consistent in their approach to due diligence. Although there were idiosyncrasies and differences in emphasis placed on their inquiries, all of them built their due diligence process as an investigation into four basic questions:

- What are we *really* buying?

- What is the target's stand-alone value?

- Where are the synergies—and the skeletons?

- What's our walk-away price?

In the following pages, we'll examine each of these questions in depth, demonstrating how they can provide any company with a solid framework for effective due diligence.

What Are We *Really* Buying?

When senior executives begin to look at an acquisition, they quickly develop a mental image of the target company, often drawing on its public profile or its reputation within the business community. That mental image shapes the entire deal-making process—it turns into the story that management tells itself about the deal. An effective due diligence process challenges this mental model, getting at the real story beneath the often heavily varnished surface. Rather than rely on secondary sources and biased forecasts provided by the target company itself, the corporate suitor must build its own proprietary, bottom-up view of the target and its industry, gathering information about customers, suppliers, and competitors in the field.

Bridgepoint, a leading European private equity firm, is particularly adept at this kind of strategic due diligence. In 2000, Bridgepoint was considering buying a fruit-processing business from the French liquor giant Pernod Ricard. The business, which for the purposes of this article we'll call FruitCo, looked like an attractive acquisition candidate. As the leading producer of the fruit mixtures used to flavor yogurt, it was well positioned in a growing industry. Western consumers had been spending between 5% and 10% more each year on yogurt, and the market was growing faster still in the developing world, particularly in Latin America and Asia. FruitCo was posting profits and had won praise for its innovativeness and its excellence in R&D and manufacturing. Moreover, there was nothing suspicious about Pernod Ricard's reasons for selling—fruit processing simply lay outside its core business.

FruitCo looked like a winner to Benoît Bassi, a managing director of Bridgepoint in Paris. He saw attractive opportunities to boost FruitCo's revenues and profits by expanding the business into adjacent categories, such as ice cream and baked goods, as well as into new channels. After laying out the case for the acquisition in a grueling five-hour meeting with his partners, Bassi got the OK to pursue the deal. Yet it never happened; just four weeks later, Bassi killed it.

During those four weeks, the due diligence team had discovered many worms in the shiny FruitCo apple. They tested the argument that FruitCo could make money by scaling up and competing on cost, for instance. And they found that while the company boasted considerable global scale, regional scale turned out to be the more relevant driver of costs. That was because the economics of transportation and purchasing made the global sourcing of fruit—a major cost component—unfeasible. At the same time, advanced processing technologies enabled FruitCo's rivals to achieve competitive economics at the country level. When the team tested FruitCo's price and revenue forecasts, they found further cause for concern. The market for fruit yogurt was indeed growing, but profitability in many markets—particularly in Latin America—was falling rapidly, indicating that the product was turning into a commodity. Stemming this trend seemed unlikely; consumers told Bridgepoint's researchers that they would be unlikely to tolerate increased prices. The team then pored over the target company's customer lists. They found that FruitCo was highly dependent on sales to two large yogurt producers, both of which seemed intent on achieving more control over the entire production process in each major market that they competed in. FruitCo seemed fated to an erosion of market power—it would have to fight for every contract.

Bassi recognized that the original business case for the acquisition did not hold up under close scrutiny. He walked away from the deal he had once coveted, probably saving Bridgepoint millions of dollars in the process. "What we thought we knew turned out to be wrong," Bassi unsentimentally explains.

As the story suggests, effective acquirers systematically test a deal's strategic logic. Like Bridgepoint, they typically organize their investigations around the four Cs of competition: customers, competitors, costs, and capabilities (often but not necessarily in that order). Within each of these areas, due diligence teams ask hard questions as they study their targets. Although they will rely on information provided by the targets, they do not accept those data at face value. They conduct their own field analyses.

Get to know the customers

Good due diligence practitioners begin by drawing a map of their target's market, sketching out its size, its growth rate, and how it breaks down by geography, product, and customer segment. This allows them to compare the target's customer segments—their profitability, promise, and vulnerability—with those of its competitors. Has the target fully penetrated some customer segments but neglected others? What is the target's track record in retaining customers? Where could you adjust its offerings to grow sales or increase prices? What channels does the target use to serve its customers, and how do those channels match your own? In researching these questions, effective due diligence teams remember always to identify the target's most profitable customers and look at how well the target is managing them. They don't rely on what the target tells them about its customers; they approach the customers directly.

Check out the competition

Good due diligence practitioners always examine the target's industry presence—How does it compare to its rivals in terms of market share, revenues, and profits by geography, product, and segment? They look at the pool of available profits and try to determine whether the target is getting a fair (or better) share of industry profits compared with its rivals. How does each competitor make the profits expected from a company with its relative market share? Where in the value chain are profits concentrated? Is there a way to capture more? Is the target underperforming operationally? Are its competitors? Is the business correctly defined? The due diligence team should carefully consider how competitors will react to the acquisition and how that might affect the business. Once again, effective teams don't rely on what the target tells them; they seek independent advice.

Verify the cost economics

Successful due diligence teams always ask the following questions about costs: Do the target's competitors have cost advantages? Why is the target performing above or below expectations given its relative market position? What is the best cost position the acquirer could reasonably achieve? The team also needs to look at the extent to which the target is using its experience in the market to drive down costs. When considering postmerger opportunities for cost rationalization, the team needs to assess whether the benefit of sharing costs with other business units will outweigh the lack of focus that sharing costs across multiple businesses might introduce. It needs to determine how low it can take costs by instituting best practices. Benchmarking can be an important aid here. It's also vital to look at how to allocate costs going forward. Which products and customers really make the money, and which ones should be dropped?

Take stock of capabilities

Effective acquirers always remember that they are not just buying a P&L and a balance sheet but also capabilities such as management expertise. Capabilities may not be easy to measure, but taking them for granted is too large a risk for any company because competencies largely determine how well a company will be able to pursue its postacquisition strategy. Acquirers should ask themselves: What special skills or technologies does the target have that create definable customer value? How can it leverage those core competencies? What investments in technology and people will help buttress the existing competencies? What competencies can the company do without? Assessing capabilities also involves looking at which organizational structures will enable the business to implement its strategy most effectively. How should all other aspects of the organization (such as compensation, incentives, promotion, information flow, authority, and autonomy) be aligned with the strategy?

In testing a deal's strategic logic, most companies will be on the lookout for potential problems—the smoking guns, the skeletons in the closets. But the due diligence process can produce nice surprises as easily as nasty ones, and it may give a would-be acquirer a reason to pursue a deal more aggressively than it otherwise might have. Centre Partners' acquisition in the late 1990s of American Seafoods, a fishing company, is a case in point. (See the sidebar "Uncovering Hidden Treasure.")

What Is the Target's Stand-Alone Value?

Once the wheels of an acquisition are turning, it becomes difficult for senior managers to step on the brakes; they become too invested in the deal's success. Here, again, due diligence should play a critical role by imposing objective discipline on the financial side of the process. What you find in your bottom-up assessment of the target and its industry must translate into concrete benefits in revenue, cost and earnings, and, ultimately, cash flow. At the same time, the target's books should be rigorously analyzed not just to verify reported numbers and assumptions but also to determine the business's true value as a stand-alone concern. The vast majority of the price you pay reflects the business as is, not as it might be once you've won it. Too often the reverse is true: The fundamentals of the business for sale are unattractive relative to its price, so the search begins for synergies to justify the deal.

Of course, determining a company's true value is easier said than done. Ever since the old days of the barter economy, when farmers would exaggerate the health and understate the age of the livestock they were trading, sellers have always tried to dress up their assets to make them look more appealing than they really are. That's certainly true in business today, when companies can use a wide range of accounting tricks to buff their numbers. Here are just a few of the most common examples of financial trickery used:

- **Stuffing distribution channels to inflate sales projections.** For instance, a company may treat as market sales many of the products it sells to distributors—which may not represent recurring sales.

- **Using overoptimistic projections to inflate the expected returns from investments in new technologies and other capital expenditures.** A company might, for example, assume that a major uptick in its cross selling will enable it to recoup its large investment in customer relationship management software.

- **Disguising the head count of cost centers by decentralizing functions so you never see the full picture.** For instance, some companies scatter the marketing function among field offices and maintain just a coordinating crew at headquarters, which hides the true overhead.

Uncovering Hidden Treasure

A COMPREHENSIVE DUE DILIGENCE effort can uncover good news as well as bad. In some cases, it can even lead a company to make a strong acquisition that it might otherwise have passed up. That's what happened when the private equity firm Centre Partners looked into buying a fishing company called American Seafoods in the late 1990s. The company caught and processed Alaskan pollock and other species from seven fishing trawlers operating in U.S. waters in the Bering Sea. At the time, American Seafoods was owned by a Norwegian parent company. But when the U.S. Congress enacted a law that made it illegal for a foreign concern to own companies fishing in American waters, the Norwegian parent was forced to sell.

Although American Seafoods' profits jumped in 1999—its EBITDA hit $60 million that year, more than double the annual average of approximately $26 million in the three preceding years—the fishing business did not, at first blush, seem particularly attractive to Centre Partners. Historically subject to wide swings in supplies and prices and under increasingly tight regulation, the business seemed fated to volatile and potentially weak returns. But when Centre Partners sent in a crack due diligence team, combining experts in consumer products, fishing operations, and marine biology, it found that, far from being a blip, American Seafoods' profit boom appeared sustainable.

The team's global analysis of the health of major fisheries turned up the most interesting data. Centre Partners discovered that the

- **Treating recurring items as extraordinary costs to get them off the P&L.** A company might, for example, use the restructuring of a sales network as a way to declare bad receivables as a onetime expense.

total biomass of the U.S. Alaskan pollock fishery was expected to grow in coming years, while the biomasses of competing fisheries—Russian Alaskan pollock and Atlantic cod, most notably—were dropping, some at a fast clip. Overall supplies of pollock and cod would fall, in other words, but the share of the market represented by U.S. Alaskan pollock would probably rise. That was good news from a revenue and pricing standpoint, and the news got even better when the due diligence team looked more closely at trends in fish prices. Although pollock prices had recently increased, as overall supplies fell, they remained well below the levels of competing whitefish like cod, tilapia, and hoki. As a result, there seemed little chance that pollock would be subject to significant price competition for the foreseeable future. The big Japanese market for pollock roe, meanwhile, remained strong while supplies were falling, leading to a sharp and sustainable increase in roe prices that seemed likely to benefit American Seafoods well into the future.

Based on the results of the due diligence analysis, Centre Partners made a successful bid for American Seafoods. It turned out to be quite a catch. Within three years, EBITDA grew to $109 million, and the private equity firm had recapitalized the company and sold a portion of its stake. Today, the firm is exploring an initial public offering. In the process, Centre Partners realized nearly four times its initial investment and retained control of the business as it sought to further grow revenue and increase profits.

- **Exaggerating a Web site's potential for being an effective, cheap sales channel.**

- **Underfunding capital expenditures or sales, general, and administrative costs in the periods leading up to a sale to make cash flow look healthier.** For example, a manufacturer may decide to postpone its machine renewals a year or two so those figures won't be immediately visible in the books. But the manufacturer will overstate free cash flow—and possibly mislead the investor about how much regular capital a plant needs.

- **Encouraging the sales force to boost sales while hiding costs.** A company looking for a buyer might, for example, offer advantageous terms and conditions on postsale service to boost current sales. The product revenues will show up immediately in the P&L, but the lower profit margin on service revenues will not be apparent until much later.

To arrive at a business's true stand-alone value, all these accounting tricks must be stripped away to reveal the historical and prospective cash flows. Often, the only way to do this is to look beyond the reported numbers— to send a due diligence team into the field to see what's really happening with costs and sales.

That's what Cinven, a leading European private equity company, did before acquiring Odeon Cinemas, a UK theater chain, in 2000. Instead of looking at the aggregate revenues and costs, as Odeon reported them, Cinven's analysts combed through the numbers of every individual cinema in order to understand the P&L dynamics at each location. They were able to paint a rich picture of local demand patterns and competitor activities, including data on attendance, revenues, operating costs, and capital expenditures that would be required over the next five years. This microexamination of the company revealed that the initial market valuation was flawed; estimates of sales growth at the national level were not justified by local trends. Armed with the findings, Cinven negotiated to pay £45 million less than the original asking price.

Getting ground-level numbers usually requires the close cooperation of the acquisition target's top brass. An adversarial posture almost always backfires. Cinven, for example, took pains to explain to Odeon's executives that a deep understanding of Odeon's business would help ensure the ultimate success of the merger. Cinven and Odeon executives worked as a team to examine the results of each cinema and to test the assumptions of Odeon's business model. They held four daylong meetings in which they went through each of the sites and agreed on the most important levers for revenue and profit growth in the local markets. Although the process may strike the target company as excessively intrusive, target managers will find there are a number of benefits to going along with it beyond pleasing a potential acquirer. Even if the deal with Cinven had fallen apart, Odeon would have emerged from the deal's due diligence process with a much better understanding of its own economics.

Of course, no matter how friendly the approach, many targets will be prickly. The company may have something to hide. Or the target's managers may just want to retain their independence; people who believe that knowledge is power naturally like to hold on to that knowledge. But innocent or not, a target's hesitancy or outright hostility during due diligence is a sign that a deal's value will be more difficult to realize than originally expected. As Joe Trustey, managing partner of private equity firm Summit Partners, says: "We walk away from a target whose management is uncooperative in due diligence. For us, that's a deal breaker."

Where Are the Synergies—and the Skeletons?

It's hard to be realistic about the synergies an acquisition will deliver. In the fevered environment of a takeover, managers routinely overestimate the value of cost and revenue synergies and underestimate the difficulty of achieving them. It's worth repeating that two-thirds of the executives in our M&A survey admitted to having overestimated the synergies available from combining companies.

Realizing that synergy estimates are often untrustworthy, some companies have made it their policy not to take potential synergies into account when determining the value of acquisition candidates. Although the concern behind the policy is understandable, such an approach can be destructive: Some synergies are achievable, and ignoring them may steer companies away from smart acquisitions. A better approach is to use the due diligence process to carefully distinguish between different kinds of synergies, and then estimate both their potential value and the probability that they can be realized. That assessment should also include the speed with which the synergies can be achieved and the investments it will take to get them.

We've found it useful to think of potential synergies as a series of concentric circles, as shown in the exhibit, "A map of synergies." The synergies at the center come from eliminating duplicate functions, business activities, and costs—for instance, combining legal staffs, treasury oversight, and board expenses. These are the easiest synergies to achieve; companies are sure to realize most of the potential savings here. The next closest circle represents the savings realized from cutting shared operating costs, such as distribution, sales, and regional overhead expenses. Most companies will realize the majority of these savings, as well. Then come the savings from facilities rationalization, which are typically more difficult to achieve because they can involve significant personnel and regulatory issues. Farther out are the more elusive revenue synergies, starting with sales of existing products through new channels and moving to the outermost circle, selling new products through new channels. Each circle offers large rewards, but the farther out the savings or revenues lie, the more difficult they become to achieve and the longer it will take. Categorizing synergies in this way provides a useful framework for valuing them. Analysts can assign to each circle a potential value, a probability for achieving the value, and a timetable for implementation, which can be used to model the synergies' effect on the combined cash flows of the companies.

It's important that this analysis also explicitly consider the cost of achieving the synergies, in both cash

A map of synergies

A deal's potential synergies are best viewed as a series of concentric circles. Those close to the center tend to be cost-saving synergies, which can be realized quickly and are likely to succeed. Those on the outside are revenue-generating synergies, which require a lot of time and management and are less likely to succeed. In determining your walk-away price, your discount factor for synergies should rise as you move away from the center.

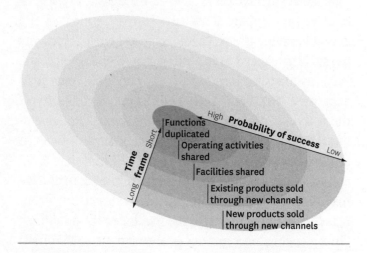

and time. In one dramatic case, the Canadian real estate companies O&Y Properties and Bentall Capital called off their planned merger in 2003 after tallying up the integration costs necessary to realize the synergies. O&Y managed properties throughout eastern Canada, while Bentall's holdings were concentrated in the West. In addition to complementing each other geographically, the two companies believed they could rationalize expenses over a larger collection of properties and still have representatives on the ground in every major

North American city. Yet, after due diligence, both sides realized that the high costs of integration would likely overwhelm any long-run savings and revenue gains. Bentall president Gary Whitelaw told the press that his company had grown "increasingly concerned that the scale of the integration could divert resources away from our primary objective. . . . The merger risks would have been significant, demanding increased management attention, and resulting in larger integration costs than at first may have been thought." The deal was scuttled, to the benefit of O&Y's and Bentall's shareholders.

It is perhaps understandable that managers might want to put off thinking about the sensitive issues inherent in integration planning until after the deal is signed and sealed. But that is often a serious mistake. Integration planning—and the costs of integration—are among the biggest determinants of an acquisition's ultimate success or failure, and you can't really declare a due diligence process complete unless you've looked closely at those costs. The due diligence team's deep knowledge of the acquisition target makes it an ideal body to develop an initial road map for combining two companies' staffs and operations.

In addition to examining the cost of achieving positive synergies, the due diligence team also needs to consider how potential conflicts between the merged businesses may sap revenues or add costs. These negative synergies—the skeletons in the closet of every deal—can take many forms. Once two companies combine their accounts, for example, some of their joint customers may curtail their purchases for fear of being overly reliant on a single supplier. Difficulties in integrating back-office operations or systems may at least briefly impede customer service and order fulfillment, leading to a loss of sales. Seeing more competition for promotions, talented employees may leave, sometimes taking customers with them. And the inevitable distractions of a merger may force management to pay less attention to the core business, undermining its results. Despite their often immense importance, negative synergies are routinely overlooked in due diligence. A common mistake, for example, is to create a valuation model that adds up the revenues of the two companies, plus the synergies, without subtracting an estimated amount for revenue erosion or increased costs.

Even the best acquirers will encounter negative synergies. An executive who left cereal giant Kellogg after its 2001 merger with biscuit maker Keebler told us that the company experienced negative synergies when it decided to put new-product launches on hold in order to focus on integrating the two companies. Some potential revenues were lost as a result even though Kellogg met its targets for cost reductions. A more devastating example of negative synergies occurred in the 1996 merger of the Southern Pacific and the Union Pacific railroads. Incompatibilities in the companies' information systems, combined with other operating conflicts, created massive disruptions in rail traffic throughout the western United States, leading to delayed and misrouted shipments and irate customers. In the end, the government had to declare a federal transportation emergency.

What's Our Walk-Away Price?

The final leg of a sound due diligence process is determining a walk-away price—the top price you are willing to pay when the final price negotiation is conducted.

The walk-away price should never include the full potential value of the synergies, which is why it's important to calculate the deal's stand-alone value separately. Synergies—especially the elusive outer-circle synergies—are something that you target in managing a completed acquisition; they should not unduly influence the negotiation of the deal unless you can be fairly certain about the numbers.

For a walk-away price to have meaning, you really have to be willing to walk away. A useful lesson in that regard comes from Kellogg's CEO, Carlos Gutierrez, who negotiated the purchase of Keebler. Gutierrez dearly wanted to close the deal. Keebler's vaunted direct-to-store delivery system enabled it to carry products to stores in its own trucks, bypassing the retailers' warehouses altogether. Gutierrez saw enormous potential for funneling Kellogg products through Keebler's highly efficient system. But Kellogg's rigorous due diligence analysis made it clear that the maximum he should pay for Keebler was $42 a share, which he expected was less than what Keebler was looking for. "Even though this was a deal that we desperately wanted," Gutierrez later recalled, "I conditioned myself mentally to say we might not have it." In a final bargaining session in New York, Gutierrez told Keebler's management that a share price of $42 was his maximum offer and that if they could get more from someone else, they should take it. Gutierrez went off to watch a Mets game, determined not to give any more thought to the negotiation. Two days later, Keebler accepted Gutierrez's offer.

To establish a walk-away price, successful deal makers convene a decision-making body of trusted individuals who are less attached to the deal than senior management is. They insist on senior management's approval of the body and establish a decision-making process that clearly delineates who in the company recommends deals, who holds veto power, whose input should be solicited, and who decides yea or nay in the final instance. They adopt formal checks and balances that rely on predetermined walk-away criteria.

Bridgepoint assembles a team of six managers, each of whom represents one of four viewpoints. One is the prosecutor, who plays the role of devil's advocate. The second is the less-experienced manager, whose involvement is a key part of his or her training. The third is a senior managing director, who no longer has any hierarchical function at the company and who therefore cannot be undermined by corporate politics. The final members of the panel are managing directors who still have operational roles. The team's goal is to provide a thorough, balanced, and unbiased examination of the acquisition candidate and hold everyone's feet to the fire on walk-away criteria. "That makes quite a balanced whole," says Bridgepoint's Bassi. "Is it perfect? I don't know. But it works."

Companies can also adjust their compensation systems as added incentive against overpaying for deals. For instance, at Clear Channel, an international radio, billboard, and live entertainment company, line managers have to sign off "in blood," as CFO Randall Mays puts it, on the cash flows that any acquisitions will deliver. The company ties managers' future compensation to meeting the division's cash flow projections, which include results from those acquisitions. The salaries for Clear Channel's M&A teams are also tied to the contribution that acquisitions make to the company's financial performance. The division presidents and M&A teams meet Mays at year's end to study all the acquisitions they have made in the previous three years to see whether they delivered what they promised and to review compensation at the same time. As Mays puts it, the deals they make "are tied to them forever."

———————

The backward-looking science of due diligence is vital. But it is a meaningless exercise without the forward-looking art of *strategic* due diligence. In the wake of so many disappointing mergers and acquisitions, more and more organizations are realizing that there are few better ways of spending managers' time and investors' money than in a careful and creative analysis of an acquisition candidate.

In the end, effective due diligence is as much about managerial humility as anything else. It's about testing every assumption and questioning every belief. It's about not falling into the trap of thinking you'll be able to fix any problem after the fact. The best private equity firms are particularly good models in this regard, since they look at every potential deal coldly, without bias or overconfidence. As Bridgepoint's Benoît Bassi puts it, "When you work for a corporation and you buy something you think is in your core business or fits with your core business, you assume you know what you are buying. By contrast, [private equity investors] have to rediscover everything. There can be a certain arrogance in corporations, which causes them to make silly mistakes." And those silly mistakes can end up costing companies millions, or even billions, of dollars.

GEOFFREY CULLINAN directs Bain & Company's European private equity practice from London. **JEAN-MARC LE ROUX,** in Paris, and **ROLF-MAGNUS WEDDIGEN,** in Munich, also work in Bain's European private equity practice.

Originally published in April 2004. Reprint R0404F

Index

above-value offers, 34
academic research, on
    negotiation, 132
Accenture, 150
acquirers
    both sides are working
        together, 161
    continually doing deals, 83
    effective deal management, 174
    learning from experience,
        171–174
    on lookout for deals, 157–158
    not seeking outside
        expertise, 27
    potential liabilities,
        knowledge of, 161
    time invested in prospective
        deal, 83
acquisitions, 65
    companies getting big fast, 68
    conflict with company's basis
        of competition, 68
    core business and, 67
    corporate managers and, 156
    counterproductive, 67
    due diligence analysis
        and, 218–219
    fine art of, 155–174
    growth strategy and, 158
    how money is made, 71
    initial negotiations in, 159,
        161–162
    keeping strategic focus in,
        159–159
    multinational food companies
        and, 71–74
    negative synergies and,
        225–226
    paying too much for, 20–21
    possibilities, 157
    price-driven process to
        negotiate, 193

quick closure, advantages of,
    170–171
transforming a business
    through, 76
revenue growth through,
    19–20
sensitivity, importance of, 156
small deals and, 81
strategic master-strokes, 76
success from making, 63
synergies, evaluating 222–226
well-established process, 156
acquisition teams, reacting
    rather than acting, 82
acrimony, isolating, 166
active listening, 117–119
adversaries, common ground
    with, 5, 14–15
agenda, bringing others on
    board, 53
aggregation, power of, 33
agreements
    changed circumstances
        and, 203
    changing terms, 189
    failure of, 86
alignment, 191
    importance of building,
        102–103
    treating as shared responsibil-
        ity, 88–89, 94, 100–103
alliances
    alignment problems, 101
    ending in disappointment, 86
    price-driven process to nego-
        tiate, 193
    signed contract and, 86
allies, enlisting help of, 49–50
alternatives, cultivating,
    166–167
American Airlines, 68
American Home Products, 161

231

American Planning
    Association, 29
American Seafoods, 216, 218–219
anchoring, as mental bias in
    M&A process, 23
anchors and initial
    valuations, 36
Andersen Consulting, 150
AOL Business Affairs engine, 93
AOL Time Warner, 65, 76, 93
applied common sense, 115–116
appreciative moves, 40, 54–61
    building trust, 55
    hidden promise, 55
    keeping dialogue going,
        43, 57–59
    negotiations, 47
    saving face, 43, 55–57
    soliciting new perspectives,
        43, 59–60
    stalemate, 59
Art and Science of Negotiation
    (Raiffa), 132
Arthur Andersen, 150
AT&T, 85–86
AutoNation, 134
autonomy vs. conformity,
    182–183
Aventis Pharma, 100

bad negotiators, 120
Bain & Company, 206
bargainers
    consensus, 53–54
    dealmaker mind-set, 87
    demands justified, 59
    dynamic of silencing, 50
    keeping dialogue moving,
        57–59
    receptivity, building, 52
    reframing process, 52

    trapped in perspectives,
        59–60
bargaining
    breakthrough, 39–61
    implementation mind-set, 87
    positions, 142
basis of competition
    achieving scale, 79
    brand strength, 72–73
    changing in industry, 76
    customer loyalty, 79
    firmly in mind, 82
    government regulation as, 77
    IMC, 74
    Internet, 79
    radio industry, 77–78
    real-asset advantage, 79
    strategy needed to
        capitalize, 82
Bassi, Benoît, 211–213, 230
BATNA (best alternative to a
    negotiated agreement), 131,
    145, 147–150, 152, 166–167
    assessing, 147–148
    court battle, 150
    inadvertently damaging, 148
    neglecting, 131, 147–149
    opposition's, 147–148
    threshold acceptable
        agreement, 147
    willingness to walk away, 147
battling over division of pie, 132
Bazerman, Max, 132
benchmarking, 215
Benetton, 196
Bentall Capital, 224–225
best alternative to a negotiated
    agreement. *See* BATNA
    (best alternative to a
    negotiated agreement)
best practices, identifying,
    29–30

biased perceptions, 151
biases
  bidding, 23
  cognitive, 20
  confirmation, 22–24
  conflict of interest, 30–31
  counteracting, 21–22, 151
  cultural differences, 22, 26–29
  influencing decisions, 19
  overcoming, 25
  overconfidence, 22, 24, 26
  planning fallacy, 29–30
  preliminary due diligence,
    21–31
  self-serving role bias, 149–150
bidding, 23, 31, 34–35
  price wars, 21
Blockbuster, 134
Blue Cross and Blue Shield of
  Florida, 107
bosses, saving face, 56–57
Boston Scientific, 34, 37
Bouw, Pieter, 185
Bradenburger, Adam, 15
brand power, 65, 69
brand strength, 72–73
breaking stalemate, 56
breakthrough bargaining, 39–61
Breuer, Rolf, 170, 183–184
Bridgepoint, 230
  predetermined walk-away
    criteria, 228
  strategic due diligence,
    211–213
brokers, agreed-upon process to
  communicate with, 100
BT (British Telecom), 85–86
building
  consensus, 42–43, 53–54
  deals on bedrock, 63–84
  on success, 71–75
Burd, Steve, 206

business
  deal management as core part
    of, 156–157
  feeding due diligence into
    planning, 163–164
  potential conflicts between
    merged, 225–226
business development
  teams, 92

Calphalon, 64
Camerer, Colin, 27
capabilities
  necessary to accomplish
    objectives, 96
  taking stock of, 215–216
  targets, 208
Cap Cities/ABC, 194
Cardinal de Polignac, 135
Career Education Corporation.
    See CEC (Career Education
    Corporation)
Cargill Crop Nutrition, 75
CEC (Career Education
    Corporation), 23
Centre Partners, 216, 218–219
CEOs
  believing in deal, 27
  companies not succeeding
    without acquisitions, 63
Chancellor Broadcasting, 77
Chapin, Mark, 54
Checchi, Al, 185
checking out competition, 214
Chen, Ming-Jer, 189
Chrysler, 181, 187, 199–201
Ciena, 168
Cintas, 83
Cinven, 220–221
Cisco Systems, 26, 134, 158,
    160–161, 168–169

Clear Channel Communications, 76–79, 228–229
clear exit expectations, 197
clinging tightly to deals, 35–38
closure
  achieving, 165
  making it happen, 168–171
  moving fast, 170–171
coach, 122
code of honor, 116
cognitive biases, 20
Colburn, David, 93
collaborating on solutions, 4
colleagues, saving face, 57
Comcast, 65, 69–70
commitment to work together to create value, 92
The Commodity Purchase, 14–15
common agenda, 46–47
common ground
  adversaries, 5, 14–15
  searching too hard for, 131, 142–143, 146
common mistakes
  failing to correct for skewed vision, 149–152
  letting positions drive out interests, 130, 140–142
  letting price bulldoze other interests, 130, 135–140
  neglecting BATNAs (best alternative to a negotiated agreement), 131, 147–149
  neglecting other side's problem, 129–131, 133–135
  searching too hard for common ground, 131, 142–143, 146
communications
  engaging with counterpart in negotiations, 99–100
  open, 55

community of practice principles, 95
companies
  acquisitions, 65
  cultures, 28
  deal making as core competency in, 127
  determining true value of, 217
  fundamental rules for making money, 63–67
  industry leadership, defining, 68–69
  investment thesis, 67–68
  major deals and, 67
  unique competitive edge, 67
comparative ignorance, 32–33
compatible interests, 130
compensation, tying to success of deal, 35
competition
  anticipating, 167–168
  basis of, 68–71
  checking out, 214
  Comcast, 70
  deal-making decisions, 68
  deals that strengthen, 71
  Harrods, 69
  MBNA, 69–70
  targets, 208
competitive
  approaches to problem solving, 52
  auctions and financial acquirers, 167–168
comprehensive due diligence, 218–219
compromises over constraints, 8–9
Concert, 85–86, 96–97
conducting audit, 190–191
confession of mutual need, 41
confirmation bias, 24

conflict
    between cultures, 27–28
    discovering hidden issues
        causing, 5–7
    of interest, 30–31
    uncovering real, 55
Congress deregulating radio
    broadcasting industry, 77
consensus
    agenda framing subsequent
        discussion, 51
    building, 53–54
conservative bias, 31
constraints, discovering and
    mitigating others', 7–9
constructive ambiguity,
    185–186
consumer loyalty, 65
contingent payment, 146
contracts
    changing terms, 189
    commitment to work
        together, 92
    as conclusion, 88–89
    dovetailing, 181
    signed, as poor indicator of
        success, 92–93
    starting point for
        problem-solving
        relationship, 182
Co-opetition (Brandenburger
    and Nalebuff), 15
core businesses, 74
Corn Flakes, 72
corporate acquirers, 155, 157
    evaluating deals
        episodically, 31
    long-term acquisition
        strategies, 172–173
    potential deals, 158
corporate managers and
    acquisitions, 156

cost
    expectations of target
        company, 208
    of not negotiating, 48
    overconfidence, as barrier
        to identifying synergies in,
        24, 26
    position, 70
    verifying economics, 214–215
counterparts, engaging before
    negotiations start, 99
Cox Broadcasting, 77
credibility and negotiating,
    108–109
crisis negotiation
    applied common sense, 114
    biggest lesson learned from,
        125–126
    dealing with criminals in,
        113–116
    roller coaster of emotions,
        117–118
    showing respect during, 114
    special skills for, 113–114
cultivating alternatives,
    166–167
cultural conventions, 27
cultural due diligence, 27, 29
cultural integration, 30
cultures
    clashing, 180, 189–191
    resistant to change, 101
    underestimating differences,
        22, 26–29, 190
customers
    getting to know, 213–214
    loyalty, 69–70, 79
    of target company, 208
cutting shared operating
    costs, 223
Cypress Group, 157–158,
    160–161

dangers
  assessing, in target
    company, 209
  of deal maker mind-set,
    87–95
Dartmouth's Tuck School of
  Business, 14
Davis, Bob, 127
deal cycle, 165
deal fever, 207
deal makers
  agreement as just
    beginning, 89
  being good closer, 92
  contract as conclusion, 88–89
  danger of mind-set, 87–95
  implementation mind-set
    and, 88–91
  M&A transactions, 127
  media glorifying, 87
  mentality, 93
  mind-set, 87, 92
  secrecy to achieve goals, 101
  wasting time negotiating
    internally, 102
deal making, 130, 137–138
  controls-based approach, 95
  core competency, 127
  glamorous, 205
  language of, 92–93
  solving growth problem, 84
deal-minded negotiators vs,
    implementation-minded
    negotiators, 90–91
deals
  alternatives to, 35
  average size, 83
  biases blowing up
    potential, 150
  brand power, 65
  building case for, 82
  building on bedrock, 63–84

capabilities needed for objectives, 88, 96
chances of good implementation, 92
clinging tightly to, 35–38
comparing with other bids, 94
conducting audit, 190–191
confidentiality of, 103
conservative bias, 31
consumer loyalty, 65
continuously doing, 83–81
decision-making processes
  and expectations, 99–100
disciplined approach to,
  80–84
discussing expectations
  before signing, 190
due diligence and, 162–164
emotion and economics, 135
emphasizing time, money, or
  reputation, 27
estimates of potential
  value, 22
existing basis of
  competition, 65
failed, 171–172
failure in due diligence,
  162–163
falling apart during implementation, 86
financial and legal due
  diligence, 82
finding differences, 143
fueling growth, 65
government protection, 65
hand-off meetings, 104–105
helping other party prepare
  for, 88
high-profile, transforma-
  tional, 75–79
humility and, 31
implementation mind-set, 87

implementation support, 88
improving implementability
   of, 106–107
integration costs, 209
interests besides price, 130
knowledge transfer, 196
lessons learned following, 171
limit price, 35
long-term strategic
   benefits, 82
making it happen, 168–171
negotiating spirit of, 177–204
planning for opportunity, 82
price, negative impact of
   focus on, 135–136
probability of success, 209
questions to ask about, 88, 96
real-asset advantage, 65
real value, 87
rewarding individuals based
   on success, 35, 106–107
rubber stamp, 31
screening potential, 157–159
social contract, 140
spirit of, 140, 199
stakeholders, 103
strategic due diligence, importance of, 210–216
superior cost position, 65
third party driving, 180–181,
   193–195
time invested in, 83
too few parties involved in,
   181, 195
transformational, 76
underlying social contract,
   179–186
valuation model, 82
walk-away price, 209
when to walk away from,
   205–230
without delusions, 19–38

deal teams, 160, 166
decision making, 40
   executive hubris, 20
   ongoing social contract, 191
   overcoming resistance in, 58
   timing and, 57
decisions, biases influencing, 19
delivery date, 8
delusions, deals without, 19–38
demands, as opportunities, 4–5,
   10–14
Department of Justice, 93
Deutsche Bank, 170, 179, 183–185
dialogue, 57–59
difficulty understanding other
   side's perspective, 133
disciplined negotiation preparation process, 106
discussions
   expectations before signing
      deals, 190
   gathering more data for, 58
Disney, 77, 194
distrustful negotiators, 10–13
divestiture, effective use of,
   79–80
Dominick's grocery stores, 206
dovetailing contracts, 181
Dresdner Bank, 170, 179, 183–185
Dresdner Kleinwort Benson. See
   DrKB (Dresdner Kleinwort
   Benson)
Dresser Industries, 192
DrKB (Dresdner Kleinwort
   Benson), 184
due diligence, 160, 162, 165
   asking hard questions, 213
   checking out competition, 214
   comprehensive, 218–219
   counterweight to excitement
      pursuing target, 210
   failures in, 162, 206–207

due diligence (*continued*)
feeding into business
planning, 163–164
final phase of, 35–38
financial side of process, 216
getting to know target's
customers, 213–214
hidden problems revealed
through, 163, 211–213
high-quality, 208–210
improving, 207–208
integration planning, 225
Ispat International, 173
management of target
company and, 163
negative synergies, 226
social contract, 194–195
stand-alone value, 216–222
strategic, 211–213, 229
synergies, 222–226
taking stock of capabilities,
215–216
target's hesitancy or outright
hostility during, 222
verifying cost economics,
214–215
verifying target's financial
statements, 205
walk-away price, 227–229
Dyer, Jeffrey, 187
dynamic of silencing, 50

earning power, 71
Earthgrains, 71
Eban, Abba, 48
economic contracts
alignment, 191
dovetailing with social contract, 195–202
embodying much of social
contract, 199–200

mutually reinforcing, 196
shared perceptions, 191
written and tangible, 195
economics, favorable, 138
effective negotiators, six habits
of, 127–153
employee ownership and target
companies, 161
End, Bob, 159
enlisting support as power
move, 42, 49–50
Enron, 36, 76
Enterprise Rent-A-Car,
67, 69
Environmental Protection
Agency, 131, 133
Equitas, 99–100
Evergreen Media, 77
executives
and basic knowledge of
negotiation, 127
clarifying role of, 161
targeted debiasing
approach, 20
experience, learning from,
171–174
experts, hiring to examine
deal, 37
explicit incentives, 42

face-to-face communication,
123–124
failed deals, 171–172
failing to correct for skewed
vision, 131, 149–152
FBI, training officers in hostage
negotiation, 112
Federal Communications
Commission, 77
Fenn, Steve, 104–105
Ferguson, Daniel, 64

filmmaking, 198–199
final agreement, and deal
    closure, 168–171
final negotiation phase, and due
    diligence, 35–38
final offer rejected, 16–17
final terms, 164–168
financial acquirers
    approach to acquisition
        process, 156
    competitive auctions,
        167–168
    success of, 155–157
Financial Times, 184
financial trickery, 217–220
fine art of friendly acquisition,
    155–174
Finn, Tom, 97–98
firm-specific language, 28
Fisher, Roger, 132, 147, 167
Ford, 188
forecasts
    differences in, 143, 146
    reference-class forecasting, 26
formal contract and joint
    venture, 178
Fox, Craig R., 32
Frères, Lazard, 135
FruitCo, 211–213

GE, 26
gearing up for negotiations,
    162–164
GE Capital, 23, 29–30
General Mills, 71–72
General Motors, 187
getting past yes, 85–110
Getting to Yes (Fisher, Ury, and
    Patton), 88, 132, 147, 167
Glaxo, 138
GlaxoSmithKline, 69

goodwill and collaboration, 96
Go Technologies, 193–194
government
    protection, 65, 69–70
    regulation, 77
Greenhalgh, Leonard, 14
growth, new products essential
    for, 71
GTCR Golder Rauner, 158,
    161, 171
Guidant, 34, 37
Gutierrez, Carlos, 72–73,
    227–228

Hanafi, Ammar, 169–170
hand-off meetings, 104–105
hard (win-lose) bargaining, 132
Harrods, 69
Hartig, Karen, 49
Harvard Negotiation Project, 86
health care, forward-thinking
    payers and innovative
    providers, 107
Helms-Biden bill, 6
helping
    opposition prepare, 94,
        98–100
    other side save face, 43, 55–57,
        125–126
Hertz, 68
Hewlett-Packard, 111, 113
high-quality due diligence,
    208–210
high-stakes negotiators, 116–117
Hitchcock, Donna, 59–60
Holbrooke, Richard, 5–7
Holtzman, Steve, 133–134, 170
HomeStuff, 8
hostile bids, 156
HP Services, 87, 108–109
Hughes, Jeff, 160–161

Huhn, Steve, 108–109
Huizenga, Wayne, 134
humility and deals, 31

IBM, 68, 167, 194
IBM Global Network, 86
IBM Global Services, 89, 104
idea sharing, importance to
   integration, 30
identifying
   must-haves, 159, 161
   red flags, 38
image and negotiators, 55–56
IMC Global, 69, 74–75
implementation
   goodwill and collaboration, 96
   mind-set, adopting, 88–91
   negotiating for, 95–107
   preparing for successful, 106
implementation mind-set, 87–91
   alignment as shared responsi-
      bility, 100–103
   vs. deal-minded negotiators,
      90–91
   helping opposition prepare,
      98–100
   managing negotiation like
      business process, 105–107
   sending one message, 103–105
   starting with end in mind, 88,
      96–98
   transitioning from deal maker
      mentality to, 94
IMS Health, 169
incentives, offering, 44–45, 48
incompatible positions masking
   compatible interests, 130
industry leadership, 68–69
Infinity Broadcasting, 77
informal messages, 166
informal negotiations, 41

information
   distrustful negotiators, 10–13
   helpful in future
      negotiations, 17
   obtaining, 18
   sharing, 10–11
initial agreement, reaching, 165
Inside Chinese Business, 189
integration, 23
   costs, 209
   planning, 225–226
   negative synergies, effects on,
      225–226
interests, 140–142
   compatible, 130, 141
   difference of underlying, 143
   of all players, importance of
      knowing,138–140
   reconciling to create
      value, 142
Internet and basis of competition, 79
investigative negotiations
   common ground with adver-
      saries, 5, 14–15
   information regarding other
      party's perspective, 3–4
   interpreting demands as
      opportunities, 4–5, 10–14
   investigating after deal
      appears to be lost, 16–17
   selling your position, 17–18
   understanding and mitigating
      other side's constraints,
      4, 7–9
isolating acrimony, 166
Ispat International, 172–174
issues, 140
   discovering conflicts over, 5–7
   most important, 12
   negotiating multiple simulta-
      neously, 11–12

offers and counteroffers, 11
receptivity to opinions and
demands, 51

Jewel, 206
Johnson & Johnson, 26, 34
joint venture, 177–178

Kahneman, Daniel, 32, 36
Kaplan, Jerry, 193
KDC (Komatsu Dresser Corpora-
tion), 192–193
Keebler, 65, 72–74, 226–228
Kellogg, 69, 72–74, 226–228
key internal constituencies,
neglecting, 170
KLA-Tencor, 106
KLM Royal Dutch Airlines, 185
Kmart, 206
Kogs, 8
Komatsu, 192–193
Komatsu Dresser Corporation.
See KDC (Komatsu Dresser
Corporation)
Kraft, 71

law enforcement negotiation
training, 112
Lax, David A., 132
LBO firms guidelines, 158
learning
from experience, 171–174
trust, 116
letter of intent. See LOI
(letter of intent)
Levolor, 64
limit price changing during
bidding, 27
LOI (letter of intent), 22

Lopez, Joe, 51
loss aversion, 32–33
Lotus Development, 167

M&A (mergers and acquisitions),
206
actively seeking disconfirming
evidence, 24
analogous situations in
companies as
benchmarks, 26
anticipating time and money
needed for, 29
aversion to, 32–33
best practices, 29–30
current basis of competition,
66–67
decision with strategic
choices, 33
executives reluctant to
pursue, 32
hostile bids, 156
Ispat International, 172, 174
leading or keeping up with
industry, 67
LOI (letter of intent), 22
managing process within
company, 80
multiple bidders, 31, 34–35
multiple possibilities, 37–38
overcoming biases, 25
overconfidence, 24, 26
preliminary due diligence
stage, 21–31
primary purpose of, 67
red flags, 27, 38
return matched or exceeded
cost of capital, 155
screening potential deals,
157–159
transactions, 127

management
  emphasis on greater account-
    ability, 95
  incentives in joint venture,
    178
  postdeal implementation,
    106–107
  rewarding individuals based
    on deals, 106–107
The Manager as Negotiator
  (Lax and Sebenius), 132
managing
  deal team, 160
  negotiation like business
    process, 105–107
manufacturers and cost
  position, 70
market multiples and price
  setting stage, 23–24
market share leadership, 68
M&A teams
  Clear Channel Communica-
    tions, 229
  pipeline of priority targets, 82
Matsushita Electric, 180–181,
  194–195
Mays, Lowry, 76–77
Mays, Randall, 229
Mazda, 188
MBNA, 69–70
MCA, 180–181, 194–195
McKinsey & Company, 20, 28
mergers, 65
  comparative ignorance as bias
    in, 32–33
  core business and, 67
  detailed written plans, 30
  drawing from past
    experience, 26
  of equals, 66
  integration in deal-making
    process, 30

  loss aversion as bias in, 32–33
  unanticipated cultural
    conflicts, 26–27
Microsoft, 150
Millennium Pharmaceuticals,
  133–134, 170
mirroring, 118
Moffett Studios, 144–145
Monsanto, 161
Moore, Don, 31
Morgan, J.P., 144
Mosaic, 75
multinational food companies
  and acquisitions, 71–72
multiple negotiation channels,
  164, 166
Murdoch, Rupert, 134–135
must-haves
  identifying, 159, 161
  Ispat International, 172
mutuality, 55

Nabisco, 71
Nalebuff, Barry, 15
NCR Japan, 180, 189
Neale, Margaret, 132
neglecting
  BATNAs, 147–149
  other side's problems,
    129–131, 133–135
negotiating
  alternative to violence, 115
  credibility, importance of,
    108–109
  evolution of research on, 132
  implementation matters,
    85–110
  large outsourcing transac-
    tions, 108–109
  multiple issues simultane-
    ously, 11–12

other side's interests, priorities, and constraints, 18
spirit of deal, 177–204
Negotiating Rationally
(Bazerman and Neale), 132
negotiating teams, limiting
people in, 164, 166
negotiation strategy, 164,
166–168
appreciative moves in, 40, 43
power moves in, 40–42
process moves in, 40, 42–43
negotiations
accepting deal, 128
achieving closure, 165
achieving scale, 79
alignment as shared responsibility, 94, 100–103
appreciative moves, 47
approaching far too
narrowly, 153
bad habits in, 127–128
benefits accruing from, 44
best no-deal option, 128
breakdown of, 111
breakthrough bargaining,
39–61
building trust, 108
code of honor, 116
community of practice
principles, 95
deal-making process, 137–138
different perspectives, 55
disagreement over terms, 1
disciplined preparation
process, 106
disclosure of background and
other information, 100
dominant party, 97
due diligence in, 160, 162–165,
206–213, 218–219, 222
exclusivity, 1–?

face-to-face
communication, 123
failure, 101–102, 112
falling into patterns, 53
final terms, 164, 166–168
flexible and respectful in, 161
gearing up for, 162–164
helping opposition prepare,
88, 94, 98–100
hostage-taker, dealing
with, 121
identifying key players, 99
ignored in, 51
implementation planning, 99
influencing process, 50–54
informal, 41
interactions, 113
interests, 140–142
investigative, 1–18
keeping the dialogue going,
43, 57–59
limiting price changes
during, 35
listening to facts, 2
long-term relationship, 87
managing like business
process, 89, 94, 105–107
negative emotions during,
120–121
obtaining information, 18
offering incentives, 44–45, 48
organizational
competence, 95
other side's motivations, 2
outside forces, 7–8
outsourcing providers and,
93–95
parity, 45
philosophy of integrity, 108
positions in, 140
power moves, 46
price, 159, 164, 166–168

negotiations (*continued*)
  process moves, 46–47
  pure price deal, 139
  relationships, 97, 108, 136–137
  right people are not involved
    in, 191–193
  risk and, 10
  sending one message, 94,
    103–105
  "shadow", 39–41
  six common mistakes, 129
  Six Sigma discipline, 95
  small agreements, 116
  social contract, 137
  solving right problem,
    128–129
  stalling, 39, 41, 54–55
  starting with end in mind,
    94, 96–98
  step-down royalties, 98
  structured auction, 167
  sunk cost fallacy, 37
  theory, evolution of, 132
  third-party advisers, 93–94
  trust during, 2, 95
  underreacting to surprising
    views, 36–37
  value produced by, 108–110
  when to stop bargaining and
    walk away, 37
negotiation teams, 108–109,
  122–124
negotiators
  acknowledging emotions,
    120–121
  aware of feelings, 117
  bargaining positions, 142
  breaking stalemate, 56
  briefing implementation
    team, 105
  building alignment, 102

  change-management and
    communication efforts, 102
  closing deals, 87
  comfortable with yourself, 117
  competitive approaches to
    problem solving, 52
  deadlocks, 1
  deal-minded, 90–91
  dismissing other side's con-
    cerns, 134–135
  distrustful, 10–13
  earning autonomy, 109
  effective, 127–153
  formal milestone reviews, 109
  gaining advantage by surpris-
    ing other side, 98–99
  good listener, 116–117
  image, 55–56
  implementation-minded,
    90–91
  informal reviews, 109
  level of objectivity, 117
  liability for deal's perform-
    ance, 109
  main objective to sign deal, 86
  negative emotions of, 120–121
  persuading other side to say
    yes, 128
  posing questions to uncover
    information, 3
  preoccupied with tactics, 149
  price bulldozing other inter-
    ests, 135–140
  raising tough questions, 97
  "reverse Midas," 135–140
  saving face, 56, 125–126
  screening out familiar ideas,
    51
  sensitivity to biases, 117
  setting up and solving right
    problem, 153

stress and, 121
terms that will cause trouble
    down the road, 97
undermining partnership's
    ability to succeed, 87
understanding and
    shaping other side's
    choice, 153
without authority, 109
working one-on-one, 121
network of trusted advisers, 30
Newell, 63–67, 69–70
Newton, Sam, 56
New York Police Department.
    See NYPD (New York Police
    Department)
Nike, 67
Nolan, Joe, 158, 171–172
Northwest Airlines, 185
Nutri-Grain bars, 73
NYPD (New York Police Depart-
    ment), 111–126

Odeon Cinemas, 220–221
offering incentives in a shadow
    negotiation, 44–45, 48
offers, multiple simultaneous,
    12–13
O'Neill, Tip, 137–138
ongoing social contract, 180,
    186–188
open communication, 55
opinions, importance of
    differing, 59
opponents
    helping prepare for negotia-
        tions, 98–100
    most important issues, 12
    understanding and mitigating
        constraints, 7–9

opportunities, demands as, 4–5,
    10–14
Orum, Dan, 182
outsourcing providers, 93–95
overconfidence, 22, 24, 26
Ovitz, Michael, 87, 181, 194–195
Oxygen Media, 182
O&Y Properties, 224–225

parallel processing, 166
parity, 45
participants holding unequal
    power, 40
partisan perceptions, 131,
    150–152
partners
    failure to fully vet expecta-
        tions, 197
    providing with incentives, 98
    relationships with, 161,
        201–202
    unspoken assumptions
        about venture's purpose,
        178–179
Patton, Bruce, 132, 147, 167
Perkins, George, 144–145
Pernod Ricard, 211
perspectives
    difficulty understanding other
        side's, 133
    importance of differing, 59
    soliciting, 59–60
Philbin, Marcia, 52–53
Philip Morris, 71
Pillsbury, 71
point of view, getting too
    committed to, 150
police negotiation teams, 122
positive working
    relationships, 130

post-negotiation reviews, 89
Post, 72
power moves, 40, 61 41, 48-50
  enlisting support, 42,
    49-50
  explicit incentives, 42
  negotiations and, 46
  offering incentives as part of,
    44-45, 48
  price on inaction and, 42
  price on status quo and,
    48-49
  reluctant bargainers and, 44
  resistance from other side
    and, 47
preliminary due diligence
  biases, 21-31
  confirmation bias, 22-24
prices
  avoiding early focus on, in
    negotiating, 159
  bulldozing other interests,
    130, 135-140
  dominating, 139
  keeping perspective, 139-140
  negotiations, 164, 166-168
price-setting stage, 23-24
price wars, 21
primary negotiator, 122
priority, difference of underlying, 143
private equity firms, 31
problems
  costs of not negotiating, 48
  counterpart's perceived deci-
    sion, 128-130
  neglecting other side's,
    129-131, 133-135
  solutions of undiagnosed, 3
  solving the right, 128-129
problem solving, competitive
  approaches to, 52

processes
  reframing, 52-53
  undisciplined, 101
process moves, 40, 61
  building consensus, 42-43,
    53-54
  negotiations and, 46-47
  reframing process, 42-43,
    52-53
  resistance from other side, 47
  seeding ideas early, 42-43,
    51-52
Procter & Gamble, 69, 87, 196
Procter & Gamble Pharmaceuticals, 97-98
proprietary technologies, 79
pure price deal, 139

radio broadcasting, 77-78
Raiffa, Howard, 132
Ralston Foods, 72
real-asset advantage, 65, 69, 79
realized synergies, 26
red flags during M&A (mergers
  and aquisitions), 27
reference-class forecasting, 26, 29
reframing process, 42-43, 52-53
revenue growth through acquisitions, 19-20
revenue synergies, 24, 26, 223
"reverse Midas" negotiators,
  135-140, 142
"reverse Midas touch," difficulty
  curing, 139
Rice Krispies, 72-73
Riley, Dan, 50
risk
  factors in social contract,
    188-195
  negotiations and, 10
Rohatyn, Felix, 135

role bias, 131
Roosevelt, Teddy, negotiation
    problem, 144–145
Rossi, Francesca, 57–58
Rubbermaid, 63–67, 70–71

Safeway, 205–206
sales, demonstrating value to, 48
Sanford, 64
Sara Lee, 71
Sarbanes-Oxley, 95
saving face, 55–57
Science magazine, 36
screening potential deals,
    157–159, 165
Seagram, 195
searching too hard for common
    ground, 131, 142–143, 146
Sebenius, James K., 132
SEC, 93
seeding ideas early, 42–43, 51–52
self-serving role bias, 149–150
selling your position, 17–18
sending one message, 89, 94,
    103–105
sensitivity to other side, 56
setting final terms, 165
SFX Entertainment, 78
The Shadow Negotiation (Kolb
    and Williams), 45
"shadow" negotiations, 39–41,
    45–50, 54–57, 61
    allies, 49–50
    appreciative moves, 54–60, 61
    leading to silence, not satis-
        faction, 40
    managers and, 40
    order of approaching people
        in, 54
    parity or equivalence of power
        in, 45

perception of mutual need
    in, 41
power moves, 61
private talks, 54
process moves, 50–54, 61
respect for another person, 57
strategic levers, 40
value creation, 48
visible creation, 48
shared perceptions, 191
sharing information, 10–11, 118
signed contracts, 92
Sittard, Johannes, 172–173
Six Sigma principles, 23,
    29–30, 95
sizing up other side, 163
skewed vision, 131, 149–152
Sky Financial Solutions, 70
SmithKline Beecham, 138
social contracts, 130, 137,
    177–204
    alignment, 191
    autocratic relationship, 203
    backlash to perceived
        breaches, 190
    benign neglect, 188
    breaches of, 190–191
    common misperceptions
        about, 202–204
    conscious efforts to shape,
        187–188
    cooperative, democratic, and
        participatory relationship,
        202
    culture clashes, 180, 189–191
    dovetailing contracts, 181,
        195–202
    due diligence, 194–195
    emphasizing longer-term,
        integrated partnerships, 201
    key provisions of, 203
    lack of awareness, 188

social contracts (*continued*)
   mutually reinforcing, 196
   ongoing, 180, 186–188
   political connotations,
     179–180
   relationships in, 202
   risk factors, 180–181,
     188–195
   shared perceptions, 191
   shared view, 203
   straightforward questions,
     187–188
   strengthening, 190
   terms of parties'
     expectations, 180
   third parties driving deal,
     180–181, 193–195
   too few parties involved in
     deal, 181, 195
   underlying, 179–186
   unwritten and
     psychological, 195
   when wrong minds meet,
     191–193
   working relationship, 202
Société Métallurgique de
   Révigny, 172
soliciting new perspectives, 43,
   59–60
solving right negotiation
   problem, 128–129
Southern Pacific, 226
Southwest Airlines, 67–68
Special K, 72
specialty chemicals, 74
spirit of deal, negotiating,
   177–204
stakeholders
   leaving in dark about poten-
     tial deal, 101
   sharing information with, 103
stalemate, 56, 59–60

stalling talks, 54–55
Startup (Kaplan), 194
step-down royalties, 98
Stonington Partners, 159, 164
store brands, 72
strategic
   alliance, 192–193
   deal making, 83
   due diligence, 211–213, 229
   focus, 158–159
   levers, 40
strategy in negotiations, 164,
   166–168
structured auction, 167
subordinates saving face, 57
success, building on, 71–75
successful deal, what to ask
   after, 171
Summit Partners, 222
sunk costs fallacy, 23, 37
superior cost position, 65, 69
superior negotiation, qualities
   of, 152–153
support, enlisting, 49–50
sustainable competitive
   advantage, 174
Sweeney, Fiona, 44–48
synergies, 207, 222–227
   achieving, 222–224
   analysis, 27
   categorizing, 223
   different kinds of, 222
   eliminating duplicate, 223
   integration costs necessary to
     realize, 224–225
   negative, 226
   overestimated, 222
   revenue, 223
   savings from facilities ration-
     alization, 223
   shared operating costs, 223
   with target company, 209

taking stock of capabilities, 215–216
targeted debiasing approach, 20
targets, 207–209
  assessing management of, 163
  assigning someone to keep in touch with, 83
  employee ownership, 161
  getting to know customers of, 213–214
  numerous bidders for, 27
  pipeline of priority, 82
  relationship with, 82–83
  senior executives compelling reason to contact, 83
  stand-alone value of, 216–222
  taking stock of capabilities, 215–216
  verifying cost economics of, 214–215
Tellab, 168
Terra Lycos, 127
third parties driving deal, 180–181, 193–195
third-party advisers, 93–94
Thomson Corporation, 79–80
Time Warner, 76
Toyota, 187
training in collaborative negotiation tools and techniques, 107
transformational deals, 76
Tréfileurope, 172
TriZetto Group, 169
Trump, Donald, 87
Trump: The Art of the Deal (Trump and Schwartz), 88
Trustey, Joe, 222
Turner, Ted, 7
Tversky, Amos, 32, 36

UN, understanding members perspectives, 6–7
underestimating cultural differences, 22, 26–29
underlying social contract
  autonomy vs. conformity, 182–183
  constructive ambiguity, 185–186
  divergent views of, 185
  failure to make explicit, 183
  implicit, 182
  no meeting of the minds on, 183, 185, 194
  real nature and purpose of agreement, 190
  scope and duration, 190
  violation of, 189
Unimétal, 172
Union Pacific, 226
United States and UN assessment, 6
Ury, William, 132, 135, 147, 167
U.S. Department of Justice, 150
Usinor, 172

Vare, Daniele, 129
verifying cost economics, 214–215
Viacom, 78
Vivendi, 65
Vivendi Universal, 76
Volpi, Mike, 134

walk-away price, 209, 227–229
Wal-Mart, 69, 196, 206
Walter, Bernhard, 184
Wasserstein, Bruce, 87
weak due diligence, 206–207

Web-based self-service
  systems, 101
Weber, Roberto, 27
Wharton's Global Chinese
  Business Initiative, 189
Whitelaw, Gary, 225
Whitman Education Group, 23
Wilson, Gary, 185

winner's curse, avoiding, 31,
  34–35
working relationships with other
  parties, 136–137

You Can Negotiate Anything
  (Cohen), 88

You don't want to miss these...

We've combed through hundreds of *Harvard Business Review* articles on key management topics and selected *the* most important ones to help you maximize your own and your organization's performance.